Babe Ruth

Babe Ruth

REMEMBERING THE BAMBINO IN STORIES, PHOTOS & MEMORABILIA

by **Julia Ruth Stevens** *and* **Bill Gilbert**

Stewart, Tabori & Chang   New York

Published in 2008 by Stewart, Tabori & Chang
An imprint of Harry N. Abrams, Inc.

TM/© 2008 The Family of Babe Ruth and the Babe Ruth League, Inc., licensed by CMG
Worldwide, www.BabeRuth.com

Text copyright © 2008 by Bill Gilbert
Produced by becker&mayer! LLC., Bellevue, Washington
www.beckermayer.com

Library of Congress Cataloging-in-Publication Data

Stevens, Julia Ruth.
Babe Ruth : remembering the Bambino in stories, photos & memorabilia / by Julia Ruth
Stevens and Bill Gilbert.
    p. cm.
ISBN 978-1-58479-697-8
1. Ruth, Babe, 1895-1948. 2. Baseball players—United States—Biography. I. Gilbert, Bill,
1931- II. Title.
GV865.R8S746 2008
796.357092--dc22
[B]
2007039415

Editorial: Amy Wideman and Kjersti Egerdahl
Design: Bryan Danknich
Image Research: Lisa Metzger
Production Coordination: Diana Ray

Printed and bound in China
10 9 8 7 6 5 4 3 2 1

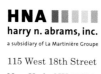

HNA
harry n. abrams, inc.
a subsidiary of La Martinière Groupe

115 West 18th Street
New York, NY 10011
www.hnabooks.com

Contents

WHEN OUR PUBLISHER ASKED US TO WRITE THIS BOOK,

I said yes immediately. It's not the first book I've written about my father and my life with him, and I hope it's not the last. I want to keep writing about Daddy because I want to do everything I can for as long as I can to preserve his memory and to make his place in baseball history and American history as prominent as possible.

Daddy was more than just an outstanding player, the best of his time and, according to many, the best of *all* time. He was also a devoted father to Dorothy, his daughter from his first marriage, and to me, whom he adopted after marrying my mother, Claire. You will read many stories in these pages that tell of his devotion as a father and the good times I always enjoyed with him. He's been gone since 1948, and I still miss him so. That tells you what a great father he was.

Daddy was a patriotic American, especially during World War II, when he made public appearances all over our nation to visit our troops and promote the sale of war bonds. Internationally famous stars like Kate Smith, Bing Crosby, Bob Hope, Irving Berlin, and many others worked tirelessly to raise money to help pay for the war, and Daddy was happy to be among them, doing his part.

He was also loyal to the sport that gave him so much. He always praised it as the best of all sports and served as its greatest goodwill ambassador, especially in his retirement years, spreading baseball's popularity throughout America and even overseas, particularly in Japan. Many sports writers credit him with igniting the popularity of baseball in that country, largely during a barnstorming trip there in 1934.

My hope is that every baseball fan will be able to relate to the stories in this book, and every devoted son and daughter, too.

Julia Ruth Stevens
Conway, New Hampshire
September 30, 2007

OPPOSITE: Babe Ruth with daughter Julia, in a photo that now hangs in her Sun City, Arizona, home.

Chapter 1

BASE BALL

BEGINNINGS

OPPOSITE: Babe Ruth, pitcher for the Providence Grays minor league team, poses for a team photograph.

HENRY FORD DIDN'T INVENT THE

automobile and Babe Ruth didn't invent baseball, but both pushed their products to new heights of popularity. Ford popularized the techniques of mass production, turning out more cars and making them available to more people than ever before. Ruth used his home runs and his king-sized personality to fire up America's enthusiasm for baseball, securing its position as the national pastime.

The list of Ruth's achievements on the field seems almost endless. His record for the most home runs in one season lasted thirty-four years; his record for the most in a career stood for forty. He hit over .370 six times, including .393 in 1923, and to this day he holds the highest slugging percentage in history: a whopping .690 (total bases divided by total at-bats). As a pitcher, his record for the most shutout innings in the World Series held up for forty-four years, and in only five full seasons he won ninety-four games and was a twenty-game winner—the pitcher's mark of excellence—twice.

His career 123 stolen bases prove the Bambino could turn on the speed on the bases as well as on the pitcher's mound.

My father was what today we would call a "superstar," and, like most superstars, he was involved in his share of controversy. However, unlike others who have experienced controversial times, Daddy was always popular—enormously so. One of the men who chased his record of sixty home runs in a season several times, Harmon Killebrew (a former slugger for the Washington Senators and Minnesota Twins), offered his explanation: "I've never heard anyone say they *didn't* like Babe Ruth. Maybe they didn't like some of the things he did off the field, or maybe on the field, too. But as far as being a person is concerned, everybody loved him."

Killebrew was speaking during a three-day seminar held at Hofstra University in 1995, on the occasion of the centennial of my father's birth. The crowd he addressed was made up of not just baseball people or members of the sports media, but also figures from a wide range of professions—scholars, poets, authors, historians, and respected experts from other fields. All of them were there to share their thoughts and analyses on my father's role in our American heritage.

In another interview at the seminar, Japanese baseball writer and historian Kazuo Sayama spoke of my father's international popularity: "He was always—he was and is—a big hero for us. And even in the war time, we felt very friendly feelings toward him. The impression of him was so strong upon us. He was always a hero."

But his most adoring fans were always the kids. Daddy had a special connection with them, maybe because he was so much of a kid himself, blessed with the same honesty and enthusiasm kids have. I think maybe it was because of his past, growing up under less than ideal conditions, that he appreciated the importance of childhood.

BELOW: The only known photograph showing Babe with both his mother and father, taken in Baltimore circa 1895. Babe's mother can be seen holding him in the front row at the far left. His father, with the mustache, pipe, and glass of beer, is sitting on the bottom step.

OPPOSITE: A three-year-old George Herman Ruth poses for a portrait in 1898.

Daddy's father, an ex-lightning-rod installer, owned four saloons in Baltimore when it was a seaport whose population included many railroad men, dock workers, and the seamen who worked on the freighters tied up in the harbor. One of the saloons was located at 406 West Conway Street, which is now short centerfield in Oriole Park at Camden Yards; the others were at 426 West Conway Street, 712 Hanover Street, and 38 Eutaw Street. Back then, horses pulled the wagons of farmers and merchants down the cobblestones of Pratt Street, through neighborhoods called Pigtown and Canton. Baltimore called itself "the Gateway to the South," with Germans like the Ruth family making up the largest ethnic

OPPOSITE: Brother Matthias, the man Ruth would later describe as the only father he'd ever had. As a teacher at St. Mary's, and the school's disciplinarian, he was among the first to witness the future "Sultan of Swat" round the bases.

"Fate stepped in during those early years when he met two men who turned his life around."

group. In 1895, the year my father was born, the Baltimore Orioles won the National League pennant for the second year in a row.

Hard times, and heartbreaking ones, seemed to stalk the Ruths. My father was the oldest of eight children, the son of George Ruth, Sr., and his wife, Katie. Of the eight children, only Daddy and his sister, Mamie, survived infancy. Katie Ruth died in 1910, when my father was fifteen.

The family lived with Katie's father, Pius Schamberger, at 216 Emory Street in southern Baltimore, where Daddy was born. His parents claimed they had trouble controlling him, but he was simply the product of his environment. As he once commented in his adult years, "I chewed tobacco when I was seven. Not that I enjoyed it especially, but from my observations around the saloon, it seemed like the normal thing to do."

His father took him to a reform school on a hot day in July 1902, when Daddy was only seven years old. In his first years at St. Mary's, he ran away three times—escapes he later called his "parole." His parents told the religious brothers at St. Mary's that he was "incorrigible." I've been told they visited Daddy only a couple of times, even though he stayed there for twelve years.

Fate stepped in during those early years at St. Mary's, though, when Daddy met two men who turned his life around. They were members of the Xaverian Brothers, a Roman Catholic religious order, and teachers at the school, but to my father they became much more than that. He grew so close to one of them, Brother Matthias, that in later years Daddy described him as the only father he'd ever had. Together with another teacher, Brother Gilbert, Brother Mathias taught young George Ruth how to play baseball.

Daddy later said, "It was at St. Mary's that I met and learned to love the greatest man I've ever known. His name was Brother Matthias. He

BELOW: Ruth (top row, far left) at St. Mary's Industrial School for Boys. The Baltimore school, run by the Xaverian Brothers, was a reformatory and orphanage that taught each boy a trade.

OPPOSITE: An image of Ruth as a sixteen-year-old at St. Mary's. He became the catcher for the school's baseball team before settling in as the star pitcher.

was the father I needed. He taught me to read and write, and he taught me the difference between right and wrong." And Brother Matthias was able to back up his teachings. He stood six feet, five inches tall and weighed 250 pounds. As if that weren't enough, he had the authority to go with his physical stature—he was the school's official disciplinarian. "He seldom raised his voice," my father said, calling it "a sharp contrast to what I had known at home and in my neighborhood. But when he spoke, he meant business."

My father was a natural athlete, the kind who can learn a sport and excel at it almost immediately. Initially Brother Gilbert made him a catcher, even though he was a left-handed thrower. Such catchers are almost

OPPOSITE: Young Ruth in catcher's equipment. Though a lefthander, he spent many of his years at St. Mary's behind the plate until he started pitching around age fifteen. He was happy just to have equipment to play with, but the mitt Ruth wore on his right hand was designed to be worn on the left.

LEFT: St. Mary's team photo, with Ruth at top center holding his mitt and catcher's mask.

unheard of in baseball: Most hitters are right-handed, which means that the hitter is likely to be in the way when the catcher has to throw to second or third base. Making things tougher yet, Daddy had to wear a mitt on his right hand that was designed to be worn on the left. But he played well at the position in spite of it—so well that when he was returned to St. Mary's after one of his periods of "parole," Brother Gilbert greeted him with, "I shouldn't be glad to see you, George, but to tell you the truth, the team needs you."

Fate stepped into his life again at St. Mary's when my father openly criticized the team's pitcher. Brother Gilbert dared him to see if he could do better. So he gave it a shot—and became the team's star pitcher.

"Mr. Dunn signed the kid they were still calling 'George,' and his fairy tale was underway."

Brother Gilbert, obviously a keen judge of talent, became so impressed with young George Ruth's development and his long-range potential that he wrote a letter to Jack Dunn, the owner of the Orioles (then a minor league team in the International League). In February of 1914, the month my father turned nineteen, Mr. Dunn visited St. Mary's to watch him play. Brother Matthias said he could hit, and when Mr. Dunn asked if he could pitch, too, Brother Matthias answered, "Sure—he can do anything."

Mr. Dunn signed the kid they were still calling "George" that same year, and his fairy tale was well underway. His first contract as a professional baseball player paid him one hundred dollars a month, six hundred for the full season.

With a career in baseball taking concrete form, Daddy left St. Mary's, but he remained close to Brother Matthias over the years. He got into several scrapes with the management of the Yankees during his years with them, and on several occasions they sent for Brother Matthias to straighten him out. My father, who was always a generous person, frequently expressed his thanks to Brother Matthias by leaving tickets to the Yankees' games for him. On two occasions, he even bought him a new Cadillac.

Likewise, he never lost his feelings of gratitude and loyalty toward St. Mary's. In later years, he remarked, "I believe it is customary for a man whose education was acquired as mine was to look back on those days either with scorn or a wish to conceal the facts. I look back on St. Mary's as one of the most constructive periods of my life. I'm as proud of it as any Harvard man is of his school."

LEFT: Babe standing with Brother Matthias. Serving as his father figure in many ways, Brother Matthias taught Ruth the game of baseball. He coached Ruth, developed his skills, and later encouraged him to play professionally.

RUTH
PITCHER
INTERNATIONAL
LEAGUE BALTO.

Baltimore. International.
1914

When he left St. Mary's to play for the Orioles, my father asked Brother Matthias if he thought he would make a good tailor, the trade taught to the boys at school, if he couldn't make the grade as a professional ballplayer.

Brother Matthias responded by saying he was sure my father would make a good tailor if he was released by the Orioles, but quickly added that he didn't think it would come to that. Predicting a successful career in the big leagues, he told him, "You'll make good, my boy, of that I am sure."

His talents showed in spring training with the Orioles as well as they did in his days at St. Mary's. Jack Dunn wrote back to Brother Gilbert, "That fellow Ruth is the greatest young ball player who ever reported to a training camp. If he doesn't let success go to his head, he'll become the greatest ball player of all time."

My father continued to merit Mr. Dunn's enthusiasm. In a spring training game in March 1914 at Fayetteville Fair Grounds in North Carolina, my father dazzled Roger Pippen, a reporter for the *Baltimore News-Post* and a friend of Brother Gilbert's who wrote, "The next batter made a hit that will live in the memory of all who saw it. That clouter was George Ruth, the southpaw from St. Mary's School. The ball carried so far

OPPOSITE: A Babe Ruth baseball card from 1914, his first year as a professional. He played for the then–minor league team the Baltimore Orioles for less than a year.

ABOVE: Baltimore's team poses in their ballpark in 1914. Babe can be seen at the far right, with an arm wrapped around his teammate's shoulder.

to right field that he walked around the bases." The next day, his name appeared in a headline for the first time—a two-column headline in the *Baltimore Sun*, no less, that read: "Homer by Ruth Feature of Game."

It was during this period that my father picked up the new name that would stay with him for the rest of his life, almost as quickly as he began drawing raves for his performances on the field. Everyone still called him George at that first spring training camp in Fayetteville when he took a spill on a borrowed bike in front of the team's hotel. According to Brother Gilbert's memoirs, the crash prompted a scout named Steinman to say, "If Manager Dunn does not shackle that new babe of his, he'll not be a Rube Waddell in the rough"—referring to one of the great pitchers of the turn of the century—"he'll be a Babe Ruth in the cemetery."

Roger Pippen heard the Scout's comment and called Daddy "Babe" in his column the next morning. The date was March 19, 1914, and it marked the first time the name "Babe Ruth" appeared anywhere.

The sportswriters covering the Orioles in spring training that year wrote that he spent a lot of time riding that bike, just like a kid. There was a reason for that: When Daddy was a kid, he never had a bike. The same explanation applies to some of his other excesses as an adult. As his career took off, he began earning enough money to afford nice clothes, something else he never had before, and good food, and a new car. Until he left St. Mary's, he had never eaten a steak, or even ridden in an elevator. When he began staying in fine hotels while traveling with the Red Sox and the Yankees, they weren't just his first stays in fine hotels—they were his first stays in a hotel, period. When he bought his first flashy car, it wasn't just his first flashy car—it was his first of any description.

In May of that first professional season, Mr. Dunn raised my father's salary to two hundred dollars a month, twelve hundred dollars for the season. Before June was out, his salary was raised again, to eighteen hundred dollars a year. At this point he was being used as a pitcher and not as an outfielder, but he was certainly performing well: His record with the Orioles for 1914 was fourteen wins and only six losses.

As it turned out, his first season with the Orioles would be his only one with them. He became so good so fast that Jack Dunn sold him that same season to the Boston Red Sox. But my father told Mr. Dunn that he didn't want to go to Boston. He said he didn't care about the money, and hated to "leave home, the school, and you."

As it was, he almost didn't leave Baltimore—it seems hard to believe now, but no team seemed to want Daddy at first. Mr. Dunn originally offered him, plus two other players, to Connie Mack, the owner of the Philadelphia Athletics. He wanted $10,000 for the three of them, but Mr. Mack refused the offer. The Cincinnati Reds also had a chance to get their hands on him, but they passed him up, too. On July 9, 1914, Jack Dunn finally sold the three players to the Red Sox. Daddy was farmed out to Boston's minor league team in Providence, Rhode Island, and was called up to the Major League team later that season. He pitched in five games and finished with a winning record.

At the end of the season, my father married Helen Woodford, a waitress he'd met in Boston. The wedding took place back in Ellicott City, Maryland, near Baltimore, and the newlyweds lived together in an apartment above the saloon owned by Daddy's father.

In 1915, my father's first full season in the Major Leagues, the Red Sox won the American League pennant. My father was still a pitcher, and

389

UNIFORM AGREEMENT
FOR TRANSFER OF A PLAYER

TO OR BY A

Major League Club.

NOTICE.—To establish uniformity in action by clubs when a player, released by a major league club to a minor league club or by a minor league club to a major league club, refuses to report to and contract with the club to which he is transferred, the Commission directs the club securing him to protect both parties to the deal from responsibility for his salary during his insubordination by promptly suspending him. Payment, in part or in whole, of the consideration for the release of such player will not be enforced until he is reinstated and actually enters the service of the purchasing club.

WARNING TO CLUBS.—Many contentions that arise over the transfer of players are directly due to the neglect of one or both parties to promptly execute and file the Agreement. The Commission will no longer countenance dilatory tactics, that result in appeals to it to investigate and enforce claims which, if made a matter of record, as required by the laws of Organized Base Ball, would not require adjustment. In all cases of this character, the complaining club must establish that it is not at fault for delay or neglect to sign and file the Agreement upon which its claim is predicated. (See last sentence of Rule 12.)

This Agreement, made and entered into this **9th** day of **July** **1914**

by and between **Baltimore (International League) Base Ball Club,**
(Party of the First Part.)

and **Boston American League Base Ball Club,**
(Party of the Second Part.)

Witnesseth: The party of the first part does hereby release to the party of the second

part the services of Player**s RUTH, SHORE and EGAN.** under the following conditions:

(Here recite fully and clearly every condition of deal, including date of delivery; if for a money consideration, designate time and method of payment; if an exchange of players, name each; if option to recall is retained or privilege of choosing one or more players in lieu of one released is retained, specify all terms. No transfer will be held valid unless the consideration, receipt of which is acknowledged therein, passes at time of execution of Agreement.)

outright, for the consideration of Sixteen Thousand, ($16,000.00)
Dollars, the receipt of which is hereby acknowledged.

It is understood that Players Ruth, Shore and Egan are to
report to the Boston American League Base Ball Club, at Boston,
Mass. on Saturday, July 11, 1914.

The parties to this Agreement further covenant to abide by all provisions of the National Agreement and of all Rules of the Commission, regulating the transfer of the services of a player, particularly those printed on the reverse side of this Agreement.

In Testimony Whereof, we have subscribed hereto, through our respective presidents or authorized agents, on the date above written:

[SEAL]   Witness: **Baltimore Base Ball Club,**

By _John Dunn_ E. H. V.
(Party of the First Part) **President.**

Boston American League Base Ball Club,

By _Joseph Lannin_
(Party of the Second Part) **President.**

Corporate name of Company, Club or Association of each party should be written in first paragraph and subscribed hereto. (See Rule 12.)

Club officials are cautioned to carefully read the provisions of the National Agreement and the rules of the National Commission, printed on the back of this Agreement, for their information and guidance.

he was a major factor in Boston's success that season. Still barely a rookie that year, he won eighteen games and lost only eight.

My father had come to Boston as a highly publicized pitcher after finishing the 1914 season with a record of twenty-four wins and only ten losses while pitching for the Orioles, Providence, and the Red Sox, but he quickly became known for a different talent. He hit his first Major League home run on May 6, 1915, and soon the home runs were flying off his bat and out of the American League ballparks. He seemed to single-handedly bring to a close the "dead ball era," when only seven or eight home runs were enough to crown a home-run champion. His slugging took a back seat to much bigger news for a while, though, as the Germans sank a British steamship, *Lusitania*, and America was swept into World War I.

But the baseball world continued to be dazzled by my father's success as both a slugger and a pitcher. Nobody else was hitting more home runs, and very few pitchers were winning more games. And here was this man excelling at both, almost standing baseball on its head. The nicknames piled up quickly as sportswriters tried to find new ways to describe the Babe: the Great Bambino, the Sultan of Swat, the Colossus of Clout, the Behemoth of Bust, and on and on. The fans were going crazy. Baseball was thriving, and so was my father. His pitching successes continued to mount. He won twenty-three games in 1916, with a league-leading earned run average of 1.75. That season he started forty-one games, which also led the league, pitched 323 and two-thirds innings as a real workhorse— and didn't give up a single home run. The Red Sox won the American League pennant and went on to the World Series, defeating the Brooklyn Dodgers four games to one. My dad pitched the second game, and it was

OPPOSITE: With his first wife, Helen Woodford. Ruth came to Boston at the tender age of nineteen, and met Helen in the same year he started his career in the Major Leagues. Though they would eventually separate, they remained married until her death in 1929.

one for the books: It lasted fourteen innings, and both pitchers went the distance. Daddy held the Dodgers to six.

In 1918, the year World War I ended, he topped the American League for the first time with eleven home runs and led the Red Sox to their second World Series championship in three years. His last homer that year came in Sportsman's Park in St. Louis. The ball reportedly bounced across the street and broke the glass display window in an automobile dealership, 430 feet from home plate.

The year held other significance, though. Three years prior, following his extremely successful second year with the Red Sox, Daddy had returned to Baltimore to visit his father at his saloon at Eutaw and Lombard streets. In 1918, his father was killed in a fight outside that same saloon. My father was only twenty-three years old.

ABOVE: Babe (center) stands behind the bar with his father, George Sr. (far right), at his Baltimore saloon.

Enclosures

BIRTH CERTIFICATE

Official document marking the February 6, 1895,
arrival of George Herman Ruth, Jr.

PLAYER'S CONTRACT

American League player's contract between the Boston American
League Baseball Club and George H. Ruth for the 1916 and 1917
seasons. The document, signed January 6, 1916, established a
per-season compensation of $3,500.

"HE HITS THE BALL HARDER AND FURTHER THAN ANY MAN I EVER SAW."

— Bill Dickey, Yankees teammate

Chapter 2

CURSE

of the

BAMBINO

OPPOSITE: Ruth makes a catch during his first season as a Yankee, on September 19, 1920.

BEFORE THE DECADE WAS OVER,

Babe Ruth's knack for breaking records was already apparent. He smashed the American League record of sixteen homers barely halfway into the 1919 season and, in September, he sailed past the National League mark of twenty-four in a season and went on to top a little-known record of twenty-seven, set in the 1880s. He finished out the season with twenty-nine home runs, and he did it in just 130 games. Meanwhile, he was still pitching; in fifteen starts, he won nine games, lost five, and pitched twelve complete games.

The nation's pastime was cast in a long, dark shadow when eight members of the Chicago White Sox were accused of throwing the 1919 World Series to gamblers; the so-called "Black Sox scandal" left many Americans disillusioned with baseball. But Ruth's extraordinary playing made it easier for the fans to forgive their beloved sport. Even to those deeply upset by the scandal, he was truly something to see; ultimately, he helped fill stadiums around the country as never before.

Unfortunately for Red Sox fans, he spent the majority of his career doing so as a Yankee.

Just when my father was achieving incredible success and helping the country fall deeper in love with baseball, his team made a move that in hindsight seems unthinkable. On January 3, 1920, the Red Sox sold him to the Yankees, of all things. The purchase price was $125,000, plus a loan of another $300,000 to Red Sox owner Harry Frazee. These were enormous sums for that time. Frazee was strapped for cash, so he felt he had to make the deal, but it wound up costing the team. The Red Sox didn't win a World Series for the rest of the twentieth century—not until 2004. That eighty-six-year drought has always been called "The Curse of the Bambino."

Frazee later explained to reporters, "The price was something enormous, but I do not care to name the figures. It was an amount the club could not afford to refuse. I should have preferred to have taken players in exchange for Ruth, but no club would have given me the equivalent in men without wrecking itself, and so the deal had to be made on a cash basis." With his talent for rising to the occasion, Daddy's first home run as a New York Yankee was against the Red Sox.

BELOW: Ruth, playing for the Yankees, smashes a ball toward the outfield during a game against the Red Sox at the Polo Grounds in 1920, the same year he was traded. He remained a factor in encounters between the Sox and his new team, frequently leading the Yankees to victory.

UNIFORM AGREEMENT

FOR TRANSFER OF A PLAYER

NOTICE.—To establish uniformity in action by clubs when a player, released by a major league club to a minor league club, or by a minor league club to a major league club, refuses to report to and contract with the club to which he is transferred, the Commission directs the club securing him to protect both parties to the deal from responsibility for his salary during his insubordination by promptly suspending him.

Payment, in part or in whole, of the consideration for the release of such player will not be enforced until he is reinstated and actually enters the service of the purchasing club.

TO OR BY A

Major League Club

WARNING TO CLUBS.—Many contentions that arise over the transfer of players are directly due to the neglect of one or both parties to promptly execute and file the Agreement. The Commission will no longer countenance dilatory tactics, that result in appeals as to it to investigate and enforce claims which, if made a matter of record, as required by the laws of Organized Base Ball, would not require adjustment. In all cases of this character, the complaining club must establish that it is not at fault for delay or neglect to sign and file the Agreement upon which its claim is predicated. (See last sentence of Rule 10.)

This Agreement, made and entered into this 26th day of December 1919

by and between ___Boston American League Baseball Club___
(Party of the First Part)

and ___American League Base Ball Club of New York___
(Party of the Second Part)

Witnesseth: The party of the first part does hereby release to the party of the second part the services of Player ___George H. Ruth___ under the following conditions :

(Here recite fully and clearly every condition of deal, including date of delivery; if for a money consideration, designate time and method of payment; if an exchange of players, name each; if option to recall is retained or privilege of choosing one or more players in lieu of one released is retained, specify all terms. No transfer will be held valid unless the consideration, receipt of which is acknowledged therein, passes at time of execution of Agreement.)

By herewith assigning to the party of the second part the

contract of said player George H. Ruth for the seasons of 1919,

1920 and 1921, in consideration of the sum of Twenty-five Thous-

and ($25,000.) Dollars *cash* and other good and valuable considerations

paid by the party of the second part, receipt whereof is hereby

acknowledged.

The parties to this Agreement further covenant to abide by all provisions of the National Agreement and by all Rules of the National Commission, regulating the transfer of the services of a player, particularly those printed on the reverse side of this Agreement.

In Testimony Whereof, we have subscribed hereto, through our respective presidents or authorized agents, on the date above written :

SEAL

Witness :

Byron Clark

BOSTON AMERICAN LEAGUE BASEBALL CLUB

H. H. Frazee
(Party of the First Part) President

AMERICAN LEAGUE BASE BALL CLUB OF NEW YORK

Corporate name of Company, Club or Association of each party should be written in first paragraph and subscribed hereto. (See Rule 10.)

Jacob Ruppert Pnt
(Party of the Second Part)

Club officials are cautioned to carefully read the provisions of the National Agreement and the rules of the National Commission, printed on the back of this Agreement, for their information and guidance.

70

While the Red Sox were beginning their long, long exile from the World Series, Daddy showed that it didn't make any difference where he played, he was going to keep hitting home runs. He contributed to the Yankees winning seven American League pennants and four World Series championships. This success was followed by even more championships for the Yankees in the eras of Joe DiMaggio and managers Joe McCarthy, Casey Stengel, and Joe Torre.

In his first year with the Yankees, Daddy almost doubled his number of homers, jumping from a record-breaking twenty-nine in 1919 to fifty-four in 1920. That year, in September, he hit the hundredth homer of his career—and he was still only twenty-five years old. He hit more home runs that year than any entire team except his own and the Philadelphia Phillies.

It's no wonder the Yankees were able to double their attendance that season, with a total of 1,289,422 fans. They became the first team in the history of Major League Baseball to draw more than a million fans in one season.

In 1921, he continued to amaze the fans, the news media, and everyone in baseball by topping himself with fifty-nine homers. Not only was he hitting more home runs than anyone else, and finishing among the American League's leaders in almost every hitting department, his smashes were still going farther than anyone else's. Many have credited him with actually changing the game from one that relied on singles and doubles and frequent stolen bases to a higher-scoring game featuring home runs. When a batter hit an unusually long home run, writers and broadcasters began to describe it as "Ruthian" in its distance, a word still often used today.

After that 1921 season, Daddy went on a barnstorming tour with the Yankees. These were popular trips in the years before television, when

OPPOSITE: The transfer contract from the Boston Red Sox to the New York Yankees that started the Curse of the Bambino. Ruth was released from the 1919–1921 seasons with Boston for $25,000—plus various other payments and loans that went undisclosed here and added up to about $425,000 in 1920 dollars.

39

teams with big league stars would travel to small towns without Major League teams of their own so fans could see the stars in person. But the next year, following the 1922 World Series in which his team was "swept" by its city rival, the New York Giants, a similar barnstorming trip wound up getting him in hot water.

Kenesaw Mountain Landis, who had become the first commissioner of baseball in 1921—after the Black Sox scandal—had forbidden players who appeared in the 1922 World Series from participating in any barnstorming trips because he felt those trips would detract from the prestige of the World Series.

Before being named commissioner, Landis served as a stern federal judge in Chicago. He ran his courtroom with strict discipline and wanted no trouble from any of the defendants or witnesses in front of him. This was the same man, after all, who had slapped the largest fine in American history to that point—$29 million—on John D. Rockefeller's Standard Oil Company; threatened to subpoena the emperor of Germany, Kaiser Wilhelm II, and have him brought into Landis's Chicago courtroom to stand trial for murdering American soldiers; and personally barred the eight "Black Sox" players from baseball for life for allegedly throwing the 1919 Series—even though a court had found them not guilty the day before.

When he began his twenty-four-year reign as baseball's commissioner, he was the same way: He was in charge, and he wasn't bashful about letting people know it.

But despite the order from "Judge" Landis, as he was called throughout his years as commissioner, Daddy played in exhibition games following the 1922 Series. When Landis found out about it, he summoned Daddy to his office. Once again, Landis displayed his willingness to

"Again he displayed his ability—almost his determination—to rise to the occasion."

challenge any violator of baseball law just as he had always challenged violators of public law.

Ignoring his "summons," my father refused to show up. Instead, he called Landis and told the new commissioner he was heading for Buffalo to play a game, which of course infuriated Landis, who promptly slammed down the telephone and yelled to anyone within earshot, "Who the hell does that big ape think he is?"

When someone told Daddy about the outburst by Judge Landis, he said, "Aw, tell the old guy to go jump in a lake." Judge Landis met the challenge by fining him his entire player's share of the World Series earnings and suspending him for the first six weeks of the 1923 season. The stern judge and the home run slugger crossed paths again that season, and Daddy seized the opportunity to ask for a pardon. Instead, Judge Landis gave him a stern lecture that lasted two hours. When it was finally over, Daddy's response was, "He sure can talk."

But while my father prepared to serve his six-week suspension, something historic was happening. In February 1922, construction began on Yankee Stadium, one of the most famous sports venues in the world, then and now. It was the first triple-decker structure in baseball, and also the first to bill itself as a "stadium." In only 284 working days, the stadium was finished, just in time for opening day.

On April 18, 1923, Daddy once again displayed his ability—almost his determination—to rise to the occasion. In this case, the opposition was, as fate would have it, the Red Sox. And—wouldn't you know it?—Babe Ruth hit the first home run in the history of Yankee Stadium, against his former team, no less. In the *New York Evening Telegram*

the next day, reporter Fred Lieb described the new athletic monument towering over the Bronx as "The House That Ruth Built," a tribute and a name still used today, because it was widely recognized that my father's tremendous ability to draw crowds made it possible for the team to finance the new stadium.

Ironically, four of the eight players in the Yankees' starting lineup for the opening of Yankee Stadium were former Red Sox players, along with six of their eight pitchers. The Boston team could not survive the significant drop-off in talent. Unlike the Yankees, on top in the American League, the Red Sox finished on the bottom—eighth in the eight-team league that season. Harry Frazee was forced to sell the team.

Daddy never let up that year in his assault on the American League's pitchers. He finished the season with the highest batting average of his career, .393, ten points behind the batting champion, Harry Heilmann of Detroit, and led the league in seven offensive departments: forty-one home runs, 151 runs scored, 131 runs batted in, 399 total bases, a slugging average of .764, 170 walks, and a home run percentage of 7.9. He was voted the league's Most Valuable Player—unanimously.

To the surprise of no one, the Yankees ran away from the Tigers and finished sixteen games ahead of them while winning the American League pennant. Then, after losing the last two World Series to their rivals, the New York Giants, the Yankees defeated them four games to two. My father hit .368 in the Series and connected for three home runs. The runner-up in home runs was Giants outfielder and future Yankees manager Casey Stengel, with two.

OPPOSITE: Depiction from February 7, 1921, of how Yankee Stadium would look when it was finally completed in 1923. Plans boasted that the stadium would be able to seat the lofty number of 75,000 occupants. Financed to a certain extent by new fans the Babe drew in, it came to be known as "The House That Ruth Built."

BELOW: The 1923 Yankees pose in their brand-new stadium, with Ruth standing at the far right.

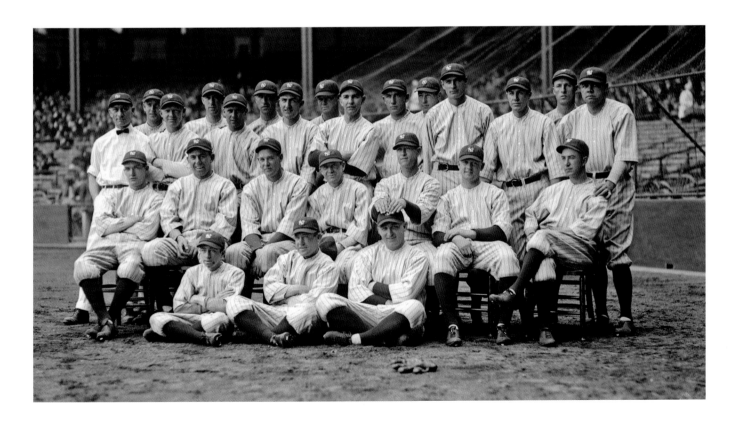

1922 WORLD SERIES TICKETS

A ticket from each of five championship games. The New York
Giants won four, with a tie in Game 2, to defeat the Yankees in the
best-of-seven match-up.

SOUVENIR PROGRAM

Selected pages from a program marking Yankee Stadium's Opening
Day, April 18, 1923. The Yankees played the Boston Red Sox and
christened their new home field with a 4–1 win.

"TO UNDERSTAND HIM YOU HAD TO UNDERSTAND THIS: HE WASN'T HUMAN."

— Joe Dugan, Yankees teammate

Chapter 3

FAMILY TIES

OPPOSITE: (From left to right) Dorothy, Claire, Babe, and Julia pose for a picture while on a family outing.

LIFE WAS A LITTLE MORE COMPLICATED

for Babe Ruth off the field. He and his wife, Helen, had been living together along with their daughter, Dorothy, since 1921, but the couple separated in 1925. Their religious beliefs prevented them from getting a divorce, and so they remained separated until 1929, the year Helen died tragically in a house fire. Thankfully, Dorothy was away at boarding school at the time. Ruth and several of his Yankee teammates attended the funeral.

A few months later, in April 1929, Ruth married the model and actress Claire Hodgson. He also adopted her daughter from a previous marriage, Julia, and together with Dorothy their family of four was complete.

started going to Yankees games with Mother and Dorothy when I was ten or eleven. From the beginning, I was aware of how much the crowd worshiped my father because he was Babe Ruth. Ballplayer or not, I worshiped him simply because he was Daddy. He married my mother, Claire, when I was twelve years old, on Opening Day of the 1929 baseball season at St. Gregory's Church on West 90th Street in New York. Someone thought it would be a good idea for them to get married early in the morning to avoid drawing a large crowd, so the ceremony took place at 5:45 a.m. As the saying goes, it seemed like a good idea at the time. The fact was, hundreds of fans managed to show up outside the church anyway.

BELOW: At home in New York City, circa 1930. Even with such a famous member among their ranks, the family regularly enjoyed spending time together at home.

ABOVE: Babe and Claire's wedding ceremony in 1929 at St. Gregory's Church in New York City. Ruth played for the Yankees against the Red Sox in the inaugural game of the season the very next day.

OPPOSITE: Babe with his wife and daughter Julia at the piano. Whatever he lacked in singing talent, he made up for in enthusiasm.

Fortunately, their marriage would go more smoothly than the Yankees' game that day, which was rained out. Instead, the game was played the next day, marking Mother's first trip to Yankee Stadium as Mrs. Babe Ruth. Perhaps in her honor, Daddy hit the first pitch he saw that day for a home run. As he trotted past third base, he tipped his cap to Mother and blew a kiss her way.

In those years of mounting baseball successes, our life at home was like the lives of most other people. Quiet times, family games, dancing in the living room of our apartment on Riverside Drive, listening to the radio in those first years of its popularity, going places together, and simply being in each other's company—that was what Daddy enjoyed most, having a family, a *real* family, where the parents and their children loved each other and enjoyed each other. Our home was so unlike the atmosphere he had experienced as a boy.

My father was an excellent dancer, probably for the same reasons he was such a superb athlete: coordination, timing, and rhythm. He was light on his feet, as they say, and he could lead a girl around the dance floor with the best of them. His favorite dance step in the 1920s and '30s was the fox trot. I was in my glory when we glided around our living room as a record spun on our Victrola. I have to admit here, though, that it's a good thing he was such a good dancer, because he sure couldn't sing. He had a good feel for the music, but he couldn't carry a tune in a basket. The dancing fulfilled his love of music.

We did so many things together as a family. We went to football games and hockey games, and we went bowling from time to time. Motion pictures were still in their infancy back then, but even as many Americans were flocking to theaters to enjoy this new form of entertainment, we rarely went. In fact, my father allowed himself to see only six or seven movies a year; for the most part he avoided them, just as he avoided reading, because he thought they might harm his eyes and damage his baseball career. We know better today, of course, but we didn't back then. My father was careful not to take any chances with his vision because of its obvious importance to any hitter.

My father used to call me "Butch," his favorite nickname for me. We shared a special routine, just the two of us, on days when he would go hunting or fishing. Like most sportsmen, Daddy liked to get a head start, so he would get up early in the morning and leave our apartment at about five o'clock to get ahead of the city traffic—as far back as the 1920s, rush-hour traffic was something to avoid.

But before setting off, he would come into my room and say softly, "Hey . . . want some breakfast?"

We'd go into the kitchen, and he would fix his specialty—a real Babe Ruth original. He would butter a slice of bread, then brown it in a frying pan. Then he'd cut a hole in the middle, then turn it over and drop an egg into it. He'd fry the egg and some bologna to go with it. And he made sure it was always bologna, not bacon.

I wasn't much of a breakfast person then, and I'm still not now, but I couldn't turn down those concoctions. They were delicious. We'd sit down and talk and eat, enjoying the early-morning quiet time together. After we finished, we'd kiss goodbye, and he would always say, "Well, thanks

> **"He was careful not to take any chances with his vision because of its obvious importance to any hitter."**

LEFT: Posing in hunting gear, the day's spoils draped around his neck. An avid outdoorsman, Ruth traveled widely to fulfill his love of hunting and fishing. His skills as a marksman made it clear that his prowess on the baseball diamond extended to other pursuits.

RIGHT: A father-daughter photo-op outside their New York home, circa 1930.

for the company." Then he'd leave for his day of fishing or hunting, and I'd go back to bed.

All the money in the world can't buy that kind of time and that kind of enjoyment with your mother or father, especially when you are as fond of your parents as I was. And that's just one example of the ways he made the bond between us strong, and made me feel that I was, without a doubt, very much loved.

Another example occurred when I was a teenager, suffering a severe case of strep throat. My condition worsened to the point that the doctors said I needed a blood transfusion. When they determined that my father and I had the same blood type, he immediately volunteered to donate, and thanks to him I was able to get over the strep throat and make a complete recovery. It was the kind of thoughtful act that Daddy seemed to perform so often, not just for me, but for all of us.

My father's favorite time of all was Christmas, probably for the same reason he appreciated so many other features of our family life: He never really experienced these happy times with his parents. Hanging the decorations, exchanging gifts, carving the turkey . . . he was enjoying all the classic holiday traditions for the first time, and enjoying them more and more with each passing year now that he had a loving wife, two caring daughters, Mother's two brothers, and my grandmother—seven of us total—all living in a handsome fourteen-room apartment on Riverside Drive in a peaceful, scenic setting along the Hudson River in New York City.

When you compare our bustling home at Christmastime with the Christmases he spent as a boy, when his parents left him alone at St. Mary's, it's hardly surprising that he enjoyed those holidays with us so much.

By far his biggest thrill was trimming the tree, which he considered both a duty and a pleasure—and his own private specialty. It was such a big kick for him that he made sure he got to do it alone. He didn't ask for any help because he didn't want any, and he was exacting about it to the point of being meticulous. For starters, he insisted on placing the icicles

BELOW: Dressed as Santa for a Christmas charity event. Ruth's delight in the holiday season, his favorite time of year, is as apparent as his compassion for children.

on the tree one strand at a time. (You can imagine how much longer that took than trying to arrange them on the tree with some well-aimed underhand tosses.)

After the tree was completely decorated, we would turn on its lights, turn out all the other lights in the room, and admire his handiwork twinkling in the dark.

My father never broke a promise to me, including his vow to attend my high school graduation. The American League schedule had the Yankees playing the St. Louis Browns in St. Louis that day, but he was adamant. When he said, "I'll be there for your graduation," I knew there were no hidden caveats.

He flew home on my graduation day, even though professional teams didn't like their players to fly because it was considered too risky in those early years of commercial aviation. He took a plane from St. Louis back to Newark, the airport used by passengers before LaGuardia and Kennedy airports were built. Dorothy and I went to the airport to meet him.

As luck would have it, the plane was late. We waited as long as we could, but I finally had to tell Dorothy, "I'm not going to graduate unless I get back to school." I made it back to Tisne, my small, private French school, just in time for the ceremony and took my seat among my classmates in the front row. I looked around every few minutes, getting more anxious with each glance, but still no sign of my father.

At last, after what seemed like an eternity, I heard a murmur starting to spread through the audience. I turned and saw Daddy and Mother coming through the door. Typical of him, Daddy was carrying a big bouquet of flowers for me. My name hadn't been called yet, so he made it there in time to see me receive my diploma.

"After the tree was completely decorated, we would turn on its lights, turn out all the other lights in the room, and admire his handiwork."

58

We wound up being the school's last graduating class. Fewer and fewer parents could afford to send their children to private schools as the Great Depression deepened and dragged on through the 1930s, and soon Tisne had to close its doors.

Dorothy and I were fortunate that we got to finish high school; there were many children who weren't able to during those difficult times. It was important to my father that Dorothy and I finish school—and earn good grades while we were there—and I appreciate the encouragement from him that made it possible for us to do so. One of the main reasons for his emphasis on this must have been that he deeply regretted his own lack of education.

I also had the privilege of going on some of the Yankees' road trips. We were in Cleveland once for a series against the Indians where my father was injured when a hard line drive off the bat of Lou Gehrig hit him in the leg. The team was scheduled to go to Chicago to play the White Sox the next day, and normally I would have gone with him to watch that game, too, except that it was July 17, my birthday, and I was hoping to meet one of my girlfriends there to see the famous Chicago World's Fair. Because of his injury, my father had to stay in his hotel room in Cleveland with his leg propped up and packed with ice to hold down the swelling, meaning he wasn't able to make the trip, much less the game. Typical of his unselfishness, however, he refused to let me miss out.

"I want you to go on to Chicago and meet your girlfriend and have a good time," he insisted. "I'll see you in a few days." I may have felt a pang of guilt about not staying there to keep him company while he recovered, but I wasn't at all surprised that he wanted me to go. His encouragement came with no strings attached, either; he simply always thought of others before himself.

Much has been said on the topic of my father and Lou Gehrig. My father loved Lou, as did all of the other members of the Ruth family. And the Gehrig family—Lou; his wife, Ellie; and the rest—felt the same way about us Ruths. As members of the same unstoppable Yankees team from 1923 to 1934, Lou and my father shared so many incredible moments; clearly there was much to celebrate between them. But their friendship suffered a blow at one point, and, as is so often the case, the cause was something trivial. Even worse, the family feud lasted seven years.

Dorothy and I loved to visit the Gehrigs up in New Rochelle, and we had a good reason: Lou's mother prepared delicious German meals and rich desserts. On one of Dorothy's weekend visits, she took play clothes instead of good ones. Before she left, I questioned her choice of a wardrobe, asking her, "Are you going to take *those* clothes?"

Lou Gehrig Day at Yankee Stadium, July 4, 1939. Mayor F. H. LaGuardia (to the right of the microphones and Gehrig) gave his respects to the hero on behalf of the City of New York. More than 60,000 fans filled the stadium to cheer the retiring "Iron Horse." The Yankees and the Washinton Senators can be seen in the infield, with the famous 1927 Yankees team in a row at right. Dignitaries and the band stand beyond the pitcher's mound.

She had a valid answer: "Yes. We're just going to be playing."

Lou's mother made the mistake of thinking those play clothes were how Mother normally dressed Dorothy. Later she told the wife of one of the other Yankee players how poorly Dorothy had been dressed during that visit. She even said something about "poor little, underfed, badly dressed Dorothy." Gossip has a way of spreading, and when that player's wife told the wife of another player, the rumor mill moved into full swing.

Of course, Mother found out about it. The wounded party always does. She became furious. Years later she told me, "I just did what any other outraged wife would do. I told Daddy that Dorothy was never going to New Rochelle again in her life." Mother made good on her promise, too—Dorothy never went back.

In Dorothy's own book, *My Dad, The Babe: Growing Up with an American Hero*, she said Daddy told Lou that his mother had said something and Lou told him, "Never speak to me again off the ball field." And so, except for their time on the playing field, they didn't talk to each other for years—and not until after Lou took himself out of the lineup in 1939. This was after he contracted ALS (amyotrophic lateral sclerosis), the disease that killed him two years later. He had to retire from baseball at the age of thirty-six.

They were reunited on Lou Gehrig Day at Yankee Stadium on the Fourth of July in front of more than 62,000 people, including Mother and Dorothy—sadly, I wasn't able to be there that day. The fans weren't there to celebrate Independence Day; they were there to say a tearful farewell. Many of the players who had been Lou's teammates, and my father's, were there, including Tony Lazzeri, Waite Hoyt, Joe Dugan, and Bob Meusel. Lou was in uniform in those famous Yankee pinstripes with number 4

RIGHT: Gehrig delivers his famous retirement speech at Yankee Stadium. Two weeks after the news broke about his illness, he stood in front of over 62,000 fans and called himself "the luckiest man on the face of the Earth."

OPPOSITE: Ruth greeting his former teammate on Lou Gehrig Day, celebrating their renewed friendship.

on his back. Longtime Yankees announcer Mel Allen was the master of ceremonies for the salute.

Mother and Dorothy knew Daddy was down there with the players somewhere, but they didn't see him, so they assumed he was either in the dugout or the dressing room. They told me they could hear the fans in our section asking each other where he was, and as they continued to look for him, they noticed that the people on the field were beginning to stir. Then Daddy came out of the Yankee dugout and walked toward home plate in a light summer sports jacket. As usual in warm weather, he was wearing a white sports shirt left open at the collar.

He walked in a straight line to Lou, who was standing near home plate, and squeezed him in a giant bear hug. Lou hugged him back, and the cameras caught the magic moment in what has become one of the most famous baseball photographs of all time. Suddenly the feud was over, and those two men who had thought so much of each other were friends once again.

Getting a kiss on the cheek from his daughter at Yankee Stadium. From left to right: Claire, Julia, Dorothy, Babe.

To this day, people ask me what it was like sitting in a ballpark and knowing that the greatest player out there on that field, Babe Ruth, was my father. I tell them I was thrilled, naturally, every time he hit a home run in front of sixty thousand screaming fans in Yankee Stadium, causing them to jump to their feet, cheering him and calling his name. How many people have experienced that thrill under any circumstances, much less experienced it over and over again? I'm still so proud of what he accomplished over the years of his career, and I was proud of every one of his many feats in every season and every game.

If he struck out and they booed him, it didn't hurt me. I always knew, even as a girl, that home run hitters strike out because the men who are pitching against them bear down extra hard to get them out, and because home run hitters take a big swing to try to propel the ball out of the park. I accepted the strikeouts as a fact of life, and knew those fans who were knowledgeable would, too. Still, when the fans booed, I'll admit there was a part of me that felt like standing up and saying, "How dare you?"

As proud as we all were of his home runs, his lifetime batting average of .342, and his seventeen seasons as a .300 hitter, including such high averages as .393, .378 (twice), .376, .373, and .372, my father was always proudest of his pitching. He was always happy to talk about his pitching records, and if someone else didn't mention them, he would.

You couldn't blame him. Before the Yankees made him a full-time outfielder to get his bat into the lineup every game so he could keep hitting

ABOVE: (From left to right) Julia, Claire, and Dorothy claim front row seats, ready to watch their favorite Yankee work his magic. The trio frequently attended games to cheer him on.

all those home runs, he led the American League in lowest earned run average, with forty-one starts and nine shutouts all in 1916, plus thirty-five complete games the next year. His won-lost percentage in the World Series is perfect: three wins and no losses. And when he beat Walter Johnson of the Washington Senators six times in nine games, he was defeating the man considered by many to be the greatest pitcher in the history of baseball. With a pitching record like that, who wouldn't mention it now and then?

John Drebinger, the baseball writer for the *New York Times,* felt the same way and said so in a 1973 story about his memories of my father. He wrote, "Great hitter that he was, he rarely discussed his astounding home run feats. He sort of felt that was something he was expected to do and what's there to say about it? But pitching or great defensive play, ah—that's something he would talk over by the hour."

OPPOSITE: Babe near the start of his career, pitching for the Boston Red Sox in 1916. In the days before his home runs made him famous, Ruth maintained a more-than-impressive record as a pitcher; he led the American League in lowest ERA before becoming a full-time outfielder.

Chapter 4

PERFECT TIMING

OPPOSITE: Ruth takes off after hitting another home run at Comiskey Park.

THE 1927 YANKEES HAVE BEEN CALLED

the best lineup in history. With future Hall of Famers Lou Gehrig, Tony Lazzeri, Earle Combs, Herb Pennock, and Waite Hoyt riding roughshod over the competition alongside Ruth, they were nearly unbeatable. In fact, they won 110 games out of 154, capturing the pennant by a whopping nineteen games over the Philadelphia A's. In the World Series that year, they swept the Pittsburgh Pirates.

Babe Ruth turned in a peak performance that season, leading the American League in slugging average, runs batted in, runs scored, home run percentage per at-bat, and, of course, his famous career-high sixty home runs—more than not just any other player, but any other team *that year. His home run record stood unchallenged for thirty-four years.*

When my father broke his own record for the most home runs in a season by hitting sixty in 1927, nobody could have guessed it would stand until 1961, when Roger Maris, a fellow Yankee, broke it. But in a way the record itself was almost predictable. Before that, he was the first to hit thirty homers, and forty, and fifty. Why wouldn't he be the first to hit sixty?

The day was September 30, and the Yankees were playing the Washington Senators in the next-to-last game of the season. It was a Friday afternoon, and there were only 7,500 fans on hand. Tom Zachary was pitching for the Senators when my father came to bat in the bottom half of the eighth inning with the score tied, 2–2. Zachary was good enough to win 186 games over nineteen years in the Major Leagues. He was left-handed—a tough match for any left-handed batter, since they don't see them as often as they see right-handed pitchers, and the pitch comes into them right off their front hip. Zachary was not a little man, either. He stood six feet, one inch tall and weighed 187 pounds, so this was no pushover that my father was facing.

He took Zachary's first pitch, a fastball, for a strike. Zachary's next pitch missed the strike zone. Then Daddy swung his way into history. He sent Zachary's third pitch halfway up the right field bleachers, his favorite target. With that one swing, he broke his own home run record, batted in Yankee shortstop Mark Koenig, and won the game.

The home plate umpire, Bill Dineen, and the Washington catcher, Muddy Ruel, agreed after the game that Zachary's pitch was an inside fastball, which my father was able to "pull" to right field. Zachary had a perfectly understandable reaction. He followed the flight of the ball from his spot on the pitcher's mound. When it disappeared into the stands, he

slammed his glove to the ground. I'm sure the reason for his angry reaction was that he realized he would be known forever as the pitcher who gave up that history-making home run.

The *New York Times* saluted the feat with the headline: "Home Run Record Falls as Ruth Hits 60th." The article, without a byline, began, "Babe Ruth scaled the hitherto unattained heights yesterday." It then described the bedlam that followed: "Hats were tossed into the air, papers were torn up and tossed liberally, and the spirit of celebration permeated the place." The paper said Daddy gave the delirious fans "a succession of snappy military salutes." Adding to the joy, the game, which was the 109th victory of the season for the Yankees, took only an hour and thirty-eight minutes.

LEFT: Caught in the act of hitting his sixtieth home run, on September 30, 1927. Ruth broke his own home run record from 1921 in the next-to-last game of the season. His record remained unbreakable for over thirty years, until fellow Yankee Roger Maris hit sixty-one home runs in 1961.

The Yankees won again the next day. Their 110 wins that season were the American League record for the next twenty-seven years. In putting on his finishing drive to break his own record of fifty-nine home runs, my father hit more homers in September than the starting lineup for the Cleveland Indians hit in the entire season.

My father's record endured for thirty-four years, but it might never have been the record at all, according to baseball historian Bill Jenkinson, a recognized authority on Babe Ruth statistics, who conducted a study of the subject that took him twenty years to complete. He wrote a book in 2006 with the intriguing title *The Year Babe Ruth Hit 104 Home Runs: Recrowning Baseball's Greatest Slugger*, making the case that my father would have hit 104 home runs in 1921 instead of 59 under the rules and ballpark dimensions that exist today.

To the best of my knowledge, nobody in baseball argued with him.

The '27 Yankees are still heralded by many experts as the greatest Major League team of all time. The lineup actually came to be called "Murderers Row" for its undeniable dominance of the league. The bullpen included Waite Hoyt, Urban Shocker, and reliever Wilcy Moore, who nabbed the top three spots in the American League for earned run average and winning percentage. The team batting average soared to .307 that year. And of course, Lou Gehrig was doing his part to add to their reputation for invincibility, hitting forty-seven home runs and fifty-two doubles, driving in a league-leading 175 runs, and winning the American League's Most Valuable Player Award. Lou hit in the "cleanup spot" behind my father, and though he may have been over-shadowed by the sustained performances of the Bambino, he was a hitting terror in his own right and was perfectly content to remain in that

RIGHT: Team portrait of the World Champion 1927 New York Yankees, with Ruth in the top row, fifth from the left. From their ranks came the batting lineup known as "Murderers Row" for its dominance at the plate.

"This nineteen-year-old kid, crude, poorly educated, gradually transformed into the idol of American youth and the symbol of baseball the world over."

fourth spot in the lineup. (Two years later, when the players began wearing numbers on the back of their uniforms, they were assigned based on a player's spot in the batting order. Daddy wore number 3 and Lou wore number 4.)

Another New York columnist, Joe Williams, wrote in that year, "Half of the time Gehrig is at bat, the customers are still cheering Ruth. [Gehrig] has been a sort of an afterthought with Yankee Stadium crowds since he has been with the Yankees."

But that was perfectly okay with Lou; as he said, "I could never be another Ruth if I lived to be five hundred years old."

Harry Hooper, an outfielder with the Red Sox when my father was playing for them, said he was almost incredulous in the face of Daddy's achievements. "Sometimes I still can't believe what I saw," he said in later years. "This nineteen-year-old kid, crude, poorly educated, only lightly brushed by the social veneer we call civilization, gradually transformed into the idol of American youth and the symbol of baseball the world over—a man loved by more people and with an intensity of feeling that perhaps has never been equaled before or since. I saw a man transformed into something pretty close to a god."

My father became such a great home run hitter that he could almost do it on demand. One game in particular seemed to prove this. The Yankees, playing in Chicago, were tied up 1–1 against the White Sox in the bottom of the fifteenth inning. The Yankees' traveling secretary, Mark Roth, was getting concerned that the team would miss its train back to New York. He began to worry even more when the railroad people came and warned him that the train couldn't be held much longer.

As my father walked past Roth's box seat on his way to home plate, he

asked him, "What's the matter with you? Sick?"

Mr. Roth said, "Yes. If you bums don't win this game in a hurry, we'll

blow the train."

Daddy told him with confidence, "Take it easy. I'll get us out of here."

Then he walked up to the plate and hit the first pitch he saw into the

right field stands to give the Yankees the lead. They got the White Sox out

ABOVE: Ruth finishing a tremendous swing during an exhibition match-up with the Dodgers at Ebbets Field, April 1927.

in the bottom of the fifteenth, made a quick change in the clubhouse, and dashed to the train station in a fleet of waiting taxicabs.

As they were hustling onto the train, my father turned and asked Mr. Roth, "Why didn't you tell me about that before?"

Harmon Killebrew, the man with more career home runs in the American League than anyone except my father, knows what it feels like to try to hit sixty home runs in one season. When that number was still the record, he made several runs at it.

"It's difficult, because when you get close to the record, the pitchers change a little bit," he told a reporter. "They don't like to see you break any records, and they try to keep the ball away from you. . . . The first year that I tied for the home run championship, in 1959 against Rocky Colavito, I was ahead of his pace for a long time, and then I had a long dry spell. . . . The pitchers seeing me hit a number of home runs tried to keep the ball away from me. So that's the thing I think that the hitters run into. And if the pitchers don't get you, the pressure from the news media will remind you every day of the record and the chase. If you're not thinking about it, they'll let you know about it. I remember reporters talking about that record. And I think then it starts to become not only a physical thing but a mental thing. You start to think about it, and sometimes the harder you try, the worse it gets and the more difficult it becomes."

"There was something magical about hitting sixty," Harmon continued. "Fifty-nine was a big number, but sixty was certainly a bigger one, and a magical type number. I remember Roger Maris when he was going

OPPOSITE: Harmon Killebrew warms up before a game he played for the Minnesota Twins. Killebrew is second only to Ruth in the American League for career home runs, with 573.

BELOW: Roger Maris, in 1961, contemplates Babe Ruth's memorial plaque in Yankee Stadium. Within a month, Maris would break Ruth's single-season home run record.

for that record, the tremendous media attention on him, and the pressure that he had was almost unbearable. . . . And I remember him saying at the time that he almost wished he hadn't broken the record."

My father's heavy bat was always a subject of discussion and amazement. It weighed 42 ounces, compared to the 33-ounce bats used by most players today. Ted Williams always emphasized that hitters should swing a light bat so they could maximize what they call "bat speed." Their theory is that the faster you can swing your bat, the harder you will hit the ball and, therefore, the farther it will go. In other words, the lighter the bat, the more home runs you'll hit.

Harmon spoke in an interview about my father, "Most home run hitters that I knew used a fairly light bat. I once picked up Ruth's bat at the Louisville Slugger Company in Kentucky, and I could hardly lift it. It was so big. So he must have been a tremendously strong individual." That's quite a statement, coming from a man considered one of the strongest players in baseball.

The Yankees' strength as a team in 1927 made that year's World Series a historic event. People said at the time that the Series was over before it ever started, and they had a good reason for saying so. Before the first game, the Pirates decided to sit in the stands at Forbes Field in Pittsburgh and get a good look at the opposition, especially after hearing so many things all season long about Ruth, Gehrig, and company, and their eye-popping power. So they went to watch the Yankees practice. That was a mistake. Daddy said later that Pittsburgh's manager, Donie Bush, "should have insisted that they go right home."

The Yankee hitters gave their batting practice pitchers a real going-over, with one long shot into the outfield seats after another. As Daddy

said, "You could nearly hear them gulp while they watched us. We really put on a show. Lou and I banged ball after ball into the right field stands, and I finally knocked one out of the park in right center. Bob Meusel and Tony Lazzeri kept hammering balls into the left field seats. One by one, the Pirates got up and left the park. Some of them were shaking their heads when we last saw them."

All of these good times over a period of years added to his enthusiasm for life. John Drebinger, a baseball columnist, said my father was "warm and friendly, with an almost outrageous sense of humor. He seemed to have only one major aim in life, to enjoy every minute of it and help others to do the same. I never met another man who was so uninhibited. There never was any acting."

Chapter 5

THE KIDS

OPPOSITE: A mob of star-struck children swarm Ruth in Vancouver, B.C., in 1926. Creating a frenzy everywhere he went, Ruth was especially beloved by children.

RUTH'S LOVE FOR CHILDREN STRETCHED

all the way from Yankee Stadium to Japan, and was known around the world—and the affection was clearly mutual. Kids clamored to be in the presence of their idol, the Great Bambino, affable and easygoing as he was. One young fan, three-year-old Ray Kelly, became close enough to the slugger to earn the unofficial title of "mascot," and he and his father were invited to join Ruth on road trips with the Yankees. Kelly was in the stands in Chicago at the 1932 World Series to witness the historic "called-shot" home run, and neither he nor the thousands of other kids lucky enough to be there that day will ever forget it.

The friendship with little Ray Kelly began when Daddy saw Ray and his father playing catch in a park along Riverside Drive, near our apartment. Daddy was so impressed by the boy's enthusiasm and his ability to catch and throw and hit that he invited the young man and his father to come out to the Polo Grounds, where the Yankees played before Yankee Stadium was built, to watch the team's next game. You can imagine the Kellys' shock and excitement. The two went to the stadium the following day and there, sure enough, were two tickets reserved for them by Babe Ruth himself.

"He left word at the players' entrance in the Polo Grounds that we would be coming," Ray said in later years, "and when we got there, we were escorted right into the Yankees dugout, and that's the way it started."

That day turned out to be the beginning of a close ten-year friendship, with Ray quickly becoming known as my father's "mascot." Ray got to sit in the Yankees' dugout before the games and make road trips with

BELOW: New York Yankees batboy Ray Kelly poses with Ruth in Yankee Stadium before a game. Ruth mentored the boy, often giving him tickets to games and making Kelly his unofficial "mascot."

OPPOSITE: Article in the "Baseball Classics" section of the *Daily News*, published June 21, 1981, examining Ruth's legendary called-shot home run during the 1932 World Series.

the team occasionally. That unheard-of privilege for a small boy gave Ray more than just a kid's unbelievable thrill. It also gave him an eyewitness seat to one of the most talked-about moments in baseball history—the famous "called-shot" home run.

It happened in the third game of the 1932 World Series in Chicago against the Cubs. The two teams had been riding each other hard throughout the Series, and some claim that my father pointed toward the bleachers in Wrigley Field and called out to the Cubs' pitcher, Charlie Root, that he was going to hit a home run to that spot.

My father was great enough to make such a bold prediction and then deliver on it, and Ray Kelly is one of those who believe that's exactly what he did. "I've read many accounts that said he didn't point to the center field bleachers, but he did," he told a TV interviewer years later. "I was sitting in a box seat right alongside the Yankee dugout at ground level, and I saw him at one point raise his hand up. Not pointing at the pitcher, but his hand was elevated.

"The first pitch Root threw to him was a called strike. And Ruth pointed a finger, as much to say, and I think he meant it, 'That's one strike.'

"Then he pitched another called strike, and Babe went 'Two,' indicating—I assume what he meant was—'That's the second strike.' And then he yelled out to him, 'It only takes one!' That I heard vividly. The next pitch was a ball, and before the next pitch was when he pointed to the center field bleachers, and following that the pitch came in, and he hit one of the longest home runs that was ever hit in Wrigley Field."

Some estimates said the ball traveled 490 feet to straightaway center-field. It was my father's second home run of the game, his last in a World

Babe wins it

Ruth's 2d HR beats Cubs in thriller

Today's installment of Baseball Classics concerns the Oct. 1, 1932 World Series game in which Babe Ruth supposedly called his home run, pointing out the spot where he would hit the ball and then doing so. As Paul Gallico's account, written in the style of his era, shows, that story is apocryphal; Ruth merely held up fingers to indicate how many strikes were on him.

By PAUL GALLICO

WRIGLEY FIELD, Chicago, Oct. 1 — The show is on — the World Series has finally clicked. In a tense, dramatic ball game full of thrills and chills and terrific cannonading, the Yankees defeated the Cubs here this afternoon for the third consecutive time in the current series. The score was 7 to 5. It was the eleventh straight World Series game the Yankees have won. One more will be a record.

Babe Ruth hit two home runs, one of them the longest ever, a smash that dropped over the wire screen into the farthermost corner of the right-center field bleachers. Lou Gehrig hit two home runs into the right field stands. In the fifth inning, Babe and Lou smashed them in succession, breaking a tie and winning the ball game with a display of brutal hitting power that let all the pep and courage out of the Cubs the way sawdust seeps out of a broken doll.

And for the final thrill, Herb Pennock, veteran pitcher who has never lost a World Series game, walked to the mound in the ninth inning when George Pipgras faltered and the Cubs rallied and, with 49,986 partisan fans rattling about his ears, calmly pitched the Chicago batters into subjection and saved the game.

The way the Cubs can get into trouble opening a ball game is simply amazing. Combs, up first, hit an easy grounder to Jurges who had all the time in the world to throw to Grimm. The Cub shortstop fired the ball right into the Yankees dugout.

Little Sewell came to bat, crouched over the plate and teased Charley Root into giving him a base on balls.

Thus, Combs on second, Sewell on first. Babe Ruth up — crack, that crack — that certain sound. Once you've heard it you never forget it. High into the center of the right field stands. Home run. Three runs over the plate. There you are, Mr. Pipgras. Go in and pitch!

George didn't start too auspiciously, either, but got out of the first with one run against him.

The Yanks lay low the next inning, although there was one pregnant smack that might have been. After Pipgras fanned and Combs flied out, Sewell teased another walk out of Root, annoying him no end, and who was at bat again? You know.

The Babe swung. Cuyler got the imprint of the rightfield fence on the seat of his pants and caught the ball. Ten feet more and it would have been a home run.

LOU GEHRIG, who had grounded out in the first, opened the third inning for the Yankees. He took his bat off his shoulder, met one of Root's specials coming in collarbone high and whipped it into the right field stands for his first home run of the game, making the score 4 to 1 in favor of the Yankees.

Now we note a Cub uprising in the last half of the third. With one out, Kiki Cuyler dumped the ball into the right field stands for a home run. Stephenson singled. Moore forced him at second but Charley Grimm hit a lashing double that Chapman, playing in right field (Ruth was in left because of the sun) misjudged off the fence. By the time he picked it up Moore had scored from first making the score 4 to 3.

In the fourth inning the Cubs sent the 49,986 addicts into hysteria by tying the score. Jurges

The Sultan of Swat.

Daily News photo

Trivia: Who came up directly after Babe Ruth's famous home run and what did he do?

Answer: Lou Gehrig, who also homered.

---

pasted the ball out to Ruth who came in like a charging bull in an attempt to take it off his shoe tops. He missed but carried the ball along with him and finally wound up sitting on it.

When he finally extracted it from beneath his person, Jurges was on second. English, next up, slapped a grounder to Lazzeri who fielded it, dropped it, kicked it, lost it and finally stood there being ashamed. Crosetti ran up behind him and made a wild throw to Dickey, pulling him so far from the plate that Jurges had no trouble scoring the tying run.

Well, we now come to the dessert, the creme-de-la-creme. This is what you have been waiting for. This is how the ball game was won. With one out in the fifth, the Great Man came to bat again. Root wound up and pitched. Strike one. The crowd booed. Babe Ruth held up one finger to the Cub dugout to indicate that but one strike had passed.

Again Root threw. Ball one. Another windup. Another pitch. Strike two. The crowd roared, yelled and cat-called. The Babe merely held up two fingers to the Cub dugout to show that there was still another pitch coming to him.

Windup. Pitch. Flash of ball! Crack! Goombye! The pellet sailed high, wide and handsome straight out for the flag pole to the right of the scoreboard in center field, where it sank into the clutching hands of the customers in the bleachers.

The Babe ran around the bases gesticulating at the Cub dugout, mocking them, teasing them and holding up three fingers. Oh, my New York constituents, how your hearts would have warmed had you seen Ruth confound the enemy.

The hubbub had not died away. The crowd had not yet settled down. The senses had not yet had time to digest the Great Man's latest miracle, when there came another sharp "crack" and Lou Gehrig, next up, had smashed his second home run of the day over the right field fence.

It blew Root right out of the game. Two home-run balls in succession was too much. Pat Malone came in and promptly walked Lazzeri and Dickey. But Chapman grounded out. Malone then walked Crosetti to get at Pipgras, and struck him out.

In the Yankees' ninth, Gehrig popped up to the infield, Gabby Hartnett carted himself, catcher's trappings and all, into the melee, galloped around in circles, bumped Jurges, bumped English, bumped Tinning. English finally managed to retain the ball.

Gabby retired blushing. Lazzeri hit the same kind of a ball high over the infield. Again Master Hartnett galloped onto the field. This time they all gave him plenty of room. He stuck out his big glove. The ball bounced in. Then it bounced out. The heat from Hartnett's blushes, this time, was felt up in the press box.

Dickey lifted a fly to Herman back of second. Herman dropped it. Chapman slashed a double inside third and Lazzeri came in with the Yankees' last run; Crosetti and Pipgras were outs.

But when Hartnett atoned for his misdeeds by opening the ninth with a home run to the left field bleachers, there was trepidation. And when Jurges hit a single into left, his third hit of the day, there was more than trepidation; there was action!

JOE McCARTHY came out of the dugout. Big George Pipgras looked in his direction and then marched off the field. And Herb Pennock heard the umpire calling him in to take up the desperate job of stopping a pinch hitter and the top of the Cubs' batting order.

Yes, here was your World Series drama, your plot and your play. Veteran pitcher called in to save game. On the train hither-bound someone asked Pennock if he thought he would get into the Series. He said: "I don't think so." Then he added wistfully, "But, gee, I'd like to just once more."

And so there he was. Rollie Hemsley came to pinch hit. Pennock struck him out. But that dangerous run was still on first and Herman and English coming up. A home run would tie it.

Herman swung from his shoulder and sent a weak grounder to Pennock, who guided it tenderly over to Gehrig. English took a healthy slash at the ball. Gehrig scuttled to his right, came up with the ball, sprinted over first base and dug the ball deep into English's middle.

That was game No. 3. There ended the drama. ∎

Yankees

	AB	R	H	2B	3B	HR	SH	SB	BB	SO	PO	A	E
Combs, cf	5	1	0	0	0	0	0	0	0	2	1	0	0
Sewell, 3b	2	1	0	0	0	0	0	0	2	0	2	2	0
Ruth, lf	4	2	2	0	0	2	0	0	0	1	2	0	0
Gehrig, 1b	5	2	2	0	0	2	0	0	0	1	13	1	0
Lazzeri, 2b	4	1	0	0	0	0	0	0	1	3	4	1	1
Dickey, c	4	0	1	0	0	0	0	0	1	0	2	1	0
Chapman, rf	4	0	2	1	0	0	0	0	1	1	0	0	0
Crosetti, ss	4	0	1	0	0	0	0	0	0	4	4	0
Pipgras, p	3	0	0	0	0	0	0	0	0	5	0	0	0
Pennock, p	0	0	0	0	0	0	0	0	0	0	0	1	0
Team	37	7	8	1	0	4	0	0	5	10	27	13	1

Cubs

	AB	R	H	2B	3B	HR	SH	SB	BB	SO	PO	A	E
Herman, 2b	4	1	0	0	0	0	0	0	1	0	1	2	1
English, 3b	4	0	0	0	0	0	0	0	1	0	3	0	0
Cuyler, rf	4	1	3	1	0	1	0	0	0	0	1	0	0
Stephenson, lf	4	0	1	0	0	0	0	0	0	0	1	0	0
Moore, cf	3	1	0	0	0	0	0	0	1	0	3	0	0
Grimm, 1b	4	0	1	1	0	0	0	0	0	0	8	0	0
Hartnett, c	4	1	1	0	0	1	0	0	0	0	10	1	1
Jurges, ss	4	1	3	1	0	0	1	0	0	0	3	3	2
Root, p	2	0	0	0	0	0	0	0	0	0	0	1	0
Malone, p	0	0	0	0	0	0	0	0	0	0	0	0	0
Gudat, ph	1	0	0	0	0	0	0	0	0	0	0	0	0
May	0	0	0	0	0	0	0	0	0	0	0	0	0
Tinning, p	0	0	0	0	0	0	0	0	0	0	0	0	0
Koening, ph	0	0	0	0	0	0	0	0	0	0	0	0	0
Hemsley, ph	1	0	0	0	0	0	0	0	0	1	0	0	0
Team	35	5	9	3	0	2	0	1	3	2	27	9	4

Yankees	301 002 001	7
Chicago	102 100 001	5

Runs batted in—Ruth 4, Cuyler 2, Grimmin 1, Gehrig 2, Chapman 1, Hartnett 1. Double plays—Sewell-Lazzeri-Gehrig, Herman-Jurges-Grimmin. Struck out—By Root4; Pipgras 1, Malone 4, May 1, Tinning 1, Pennock 1. Bases on balls—Off Root 3, Pipgras 3, Malone 4. Hit by pitcher—by May (Sewell). Hits—Off Root 6 in 4½ innings; Malone 1 in 2½ innings; May 1 in 1½ innings, Pipgras 9 in 8 (none out in ninth). Winning pitcher—Pipgras. Losing pitcher—Root. Left on bases—Chicago 6, New York 8. Time—2:11. Umpires—Van Graflan (AL) at the plate; Magerkurth (NL), first base; Dinneen(AL), second base; Klein (NL), third base. Attendance: 49,986.

Series game, and it became one of the most memorable moments in World Series history. It would also become one of the most widely debated.

In the *New York Daily News* the next morning, October 2, reporter Paul Gallico told his readers that my father "pointed to the spot where he expected to send his rapier home." Another New York newspaper, the *World-Telegram,* ran a headline that read: "Ruth Calls Shot as He Points—Homer No. 2 in the Side Pocket."

The arguments began immediately. The Associated Press didn't give any credibility to the notion that the shot was predicted. "The Babe held up one finger and finally two on each hand, with the count two and two," the AP reported. "Then, wham! He caught Root's next pitch and they never got the ball back. . . . As he trotted around the bags he held up four fingers, signifying a home run."

Oddly enough, as if to make the home run even more controversial, at least two prominent newspapers, the *Chicago Tribune* and the *Sporting News*, which used to call itself "the bible of baseball," didn't even mention the controversy at the time. Instead, the *Sporting News* waited until 1944 to pick up on the enduring argument, devoting a full page to an article titled "My Greatest Diamond Thrill"—my father's version of the legend, as told to John P. Carmichael of the *Chicago Daily News.*

Bill Deane, a former senior research associate for the National Baseball Library at the Baseball Hall of Fame and an authority on baseball history and records, wrote a lengthy magazine article on the subject sixty-one years later. He quoted players, writers, and broadcasters who were at the game, as well as my father. He said my father told Cubs catcher Gabby Hartnett, "If that bum [Charlie Root] throws one in here, I'll hit it over the fence again."

MY GREATEST DIAMOND THRILL

By Babe Ruth, Retired Sultan of Swat,

As Told to John P. Carmichael of the Chicago Daily News

'Calling Shot Foolish--But It Felt Great'

Babe Said to Himself 'You Lucky, Lucky Bum,' as He Ran Around Bases

Nobody but a blankety-blank fool would-a done what I did that day. When I think of what-a idiot I'd a been if I'd struck out and I could-a, too, just as well as not because I was mad and I'd made up my mind to swing at the next pitch if I could reach it with a bat. Boy, when I think of the good breaks in my life. . . . that was one of 'em!

Aw, everybody knows that game: the day I hit the homer off ol' Charlie Root there in Wrigley Field, the day (October 1), the third game of that 1932 World's Series. But right now I want to settle all arguments: I didn't exactly point to any spot, like the flagpole. Anyway, I didn't mean to. I just sorta waved at the whole fence, but that was *foolish enough*. All I wanted to do was give that thing a ride . . . outta the park . . . anywhere.

I used to pop off a lot about hittin' homers, but *mostly* among us Yankees. Combs and Fletcher and Crosetti and all of 'em used to holler at me when I'd pick up a bat in a close game: "Come on, Babe, hit one."

'Member Herb Pennock? He was a great pitcher, believe me! He told me once: "Babe, I get the biggest thrill of my life whenever I see you hit a home run. It's just like watchin' a circus act."

Always Fun for the Babe

So I'd often kid 'em back and say: "O. K., you bums . . . I'll hit one." Sometimes I did; sometimes I didn't . . . but what the heck, it was fun.

One day we were playin' in Chicago against the White Sox and Mark Roth, our secretary, was worryin' about holdin' the train because we were in extra innings. He was fidgetin' around behind the dugout, lookin' at his watch, and I saw him when I went up to hit in the fifteenth. "All right, quit worrying," I told him. "I'll get this over with right now." Mike Cvengros was pitchin' and I hit one outta the park. We made the train easy. It was fun.

I'd had a lot of trouble in '32 and we weren't any cinches to win that pennant, either, 'cause old Mose Grove was *tryin'* to keep the Athletics up there for their fourth straight flag and sometime in June I pulled a muscle in my right leg chasin' a fly ball. I was on the bench about three weeks and when I started to play again I had to wear a rubber bandage from my hip to my knee. You know, the ole Babe wasn't gettin' any younger and Foxx was ahead of me in homers. I was 11 behind him early in September and never did catch up. I wouldn't get one good ball a series to swing at. I remember one whole week when I'll bet I was walked four times in every game.

I always had three ambitions: I wanted *to play 20 years in the big leagues.* I wanted to play in ten *World's Series,* and I wanted to hit 700 home runs. Well, '32 was one away from my *twentieth* year and that series with the Cubs was No. 10 and I finally wound up with 729 *home* runs, countin' World's Series games, so I can't kick. But then along *in September* I had to quit the club and go home because my stomach was kickin' up and the docs found out my appendix was inflamed and maybe I'd have to have it out. No, sir, I wouldn't let 'em . . . not till after the season anyway.

Players' Riding OK, But Andy? Ugh!

The World's Series didn't last long, but it was *a* honey. That Malone and that Grimes didn't talk like any Sunday School guys, and their trainer . . . yeah, Andy Lotshaw . . . he got smart in the first game at New York, too. That's what started me off. I popped up *once* in that one, and he was on their bench wavin' a towel at me and hollerin': "If I had you, I'd hitch you to a wagon, you pot-belly." I didn't mind no ball players yellin' at me, but the trainer cuttin' in . . . that made me sore. As long as they started in on me, we let 'em have it. We went after 'em and maybe we gave 'em more than they could take, 'cause they looked beat before they went off the field.

We didn't have to do much the first game at home. Guy Bush walked everybody around the bases. Anyway, we got into Chicago for the third game and that's where those Cubs decided to really get on us. They were in front of their home town folks and I guess they thought they better act tough. I'd never been in Wrigley Field before, but in batting practice I hit nine balls into them bleachers . . . some into the extra stands behind the fence. I saw a couple of the Cubs standin' around with mouths *open* and I yelled: "I'd play for half my salary if I could hit in this dump all my *life.*"

We were givin' them (the Cubs) hell about how *cheap* they were to Mark Koenig, *only votin'* him a half-share in the Series, and *they were callin'* me big-belly and balloon-head, but I think we had 'em madder *by givin'* them that ol' Jump-in-the-throat sign . . . you know, the thumb and finger at the windpipe. That's like *callin'* a guy yellow. Then in the very first inning I got a hold of one with two on and parked *it* in the *stands for a* three-run lead and that shut 'em up pretty well. But they came back and we were tied 4 to 4 going into the fifth frame.

You know another thing I think of in that game was the play Jurges made on *Joe* Sewell in that fifth . . . just ahead of me. I was out there waitin' to hit, so I could see it good and he made a helluva pickup, way back on the grass, and "shot" Joe out by a half-step. I didn't know whether they were gonna get on me or not when I got to the box, but I saw a lemon rolling out to the plate and I looked over and there was Malone and *Grimes* with their thumbs in their ears, wiggling their fingers at me.

I told Hartnett: "If that bum (Root) throws one in here, I'll hit it over the fence again," and I'll say for Gabby, he didn't answer, but those *other guys* were standing in the dugout, cocky because they'd got four runs back and everybody hollerin'. *So* I just changed my mind. I took two strikes and after each one I *held* up my finger and said: "That's one" and "That's two." Ask Gabby . . . he could hear me. Then's when I waved to the fence!

No, I didn't point to any spot, but as long as I'd called the first two strikes on myself, I hadda go through with it. It was damned foolishness, sure, but I just felt like *doing it* and I felt pretty sure Root would put one close enough for me to cut at, because I was showin' him up too, wasn't I? What the hell, he hadda take a chance as well as I did or walk me.

Gosh, that was a great feelin' . . . gettin' a hold of that ball and I knew it was going someplace . . . yes, sir, you can feel it in your hands when you've laid wood on one. How that mob howled. Me? I just laughed . . . laughed to myself going around the bases and thinking: "You lucky bum . . . lucky, lucky," and I looked at poor Charlie (Root) watchin' me and then I saw Art Fletcher (Yankee coach) at third wavin' his cap and behind him I could see the Cubs and I just stopped on third and laughed out loud and slapped my knees and yelled: "Squeeze-the-Eagle-Club" so they'd know I was referrin' to Koenig and for special to Malone I called him "meat-head" and asked when he was gonna pitch.

Yeah, it was silly. I was a blankety-blank fool. But I got away with it and after Gehrig homered, behind me, their backs were broken.

That was a day they're still talking about.

Babe's Biggest Boot

Here is the box score of the World's Series game, October 1, 1932, that gave Babe Ruth his greatest diamond thrill:

New York.	AB.	R.	H.	O.	A.	E.
Combs, cf	5	1	0	1	0	0
Sewell, 3b	2	1	0	2	2	0
RUTH, lf	4	2	2	2	0	0
Gehrig, 1b	5	2	2	13	1	0
Lazzeri, 2b	4	1	0	3	4	1
Dickey, c	4	0	1	2	1	0
Chapman, rf	4	0	2	0	0	0
Crosetti, ss	4	0	1	4	4	0
Pipgras, p	5	0	0	0	0	0
Pennock, p	0	0	0	0	1	0
Totals	37	7	8	27	13	1

Chicago	AB.	R.	H.	O.	A.	E.
Herman, 2b	4	1	0	1	2	1
English, 3b	4	0	0	0	3	0
Cuyler, rf	4	1	3	1	0	0
Stephenson, lf	4	0	1	1	0	0
Moore, cf	3	1	0	3	0	0
Grimm, 1b	4	0	1	8	0	0
Hartnett, c	4	1	1	10	1	1
Jurges, ss	4	1	3	3	3	2
Root, p	2	0	0	0	0	0
Malone, p	0	0	0	0	0	0
May, p	0	0	0	0	0	0
Tinning, p	0	0	0	0	0	0
*Gudat	1	0	0	0	0	0
†Koenig	0	0	0	0	0	0
‡Hemsley	1	0	0	0	0	0
Totals	35	5	9	27	9	4

*Batted for Malone in seventh.
†Batted for Tinning in ninth.
‡Batted for Koenig in ninth.

New York	301	020	001	—7
Chicago	102	100	001	—5

Runs batted in—RUTH 4, Gehrig 2, Cuyler 2, Grimm, Chapman, Hartnett. Two-base hits—Chapman, Cuyler, Jurges, Grimm. Home runs—RUTH 2, Gehrig 2, Cuyler, Hartnett. Stolen base—Jurges. Double plays—Sewell, Lazzeri and Gehrig; Herman, Jurges and Grimm. Struck out—By Root 4, by Malone 4, by May 1, by Tinning 1, by Pipgras 1, by Pennock 1. Bases on balls—Off Root 3, off Malone 4, off Pipgras 3. Hit by pitcher—By May 1. Hits—Off Root 6 in 4 1-3 innings, off Malone 1 in 2 2-3 innings, off May 1 in 1 2-3 innings, off Tinning 0 in 2-3 inning, off Pipgras 9 in 8 innings, off Pennock 0 in 1 inning. Winning pitcher Pipgras. Losing pitcher—Root. Umpires—Van Graflan (A. L.), Magerkurth (N. L.), Dinneen (A. L.) and Klem (N. L.). Time—2:11. Attendance—49,986.

Picks on Close One

"I FELT sure Root would put one close . . ."

Babe Had Other Homer Thrills in World's Series

Although Babe Ruth's called home run shot in the 1932 Yankee-Cub World's Series gave the big guy his *greatest* thrill, the *Bambino* also had two real thrill days in Yankee *World's* Series battles with the Cardinals. Twice at Sportsman's Park, *St. Louis,* when he hung a pall over the hopes of Redbird fans by knocking out three home runs *in* a game. In the fourth game of the *1926 Series—October 6,* which the Yankees won, 10 to 5, Ruth crashed out three *homers in successive times* at bat, two off Flint Rhem and a third off Herman Bell. The latter was the longest home run wallop ever seen in the St. Louis park.

Two years later, October 9, 1928, in the fourth game of the second Yankee-Cardinal Series, Babe pasted Willie Sherdel for two merry-go-round rides and Alexander for the third, the Yankees winning, 7 to 3.

Oddly enough, in Ruth's long career, as a circuit clouter, he enjoyed only two three-homer *games* in league play.

"YOU CAN feel it when you *lay* wood on one . . ."

'No One Point, But Out There'

BABE RUTH CALLING his home run shot in Wrigley Field, Chicago, during 1932 World's Series. "I just sorta waved at the whole fence," he says.

"How that mob howled!"

Next—Dodgers' Big Deal With Cards for Medwick

At the 1938 All-Star game in Cincinnati, *Larry* MacPhail, then president of the Dodgers, first made overtures to Sam Breadon, head of St. Louis' Cardinals, for the purchase *of* Joe Medwick, crack left fielder of the Redbirds. It was nearly two years later, June 12, 1940, that the deal finally was completed *in* Breadon's St. Louis home, as Larry and Branch Rickey, then *vice-president* of the Cardinals, argued far into the night on "what Brooklyn players would accompany the $125,000 which MacPhail agreed *to turn over* for Medwick and Pitcher Curt Davis.

In next week's issue, Frederick G. Lieb will relate the inside story of this famous deal—one of the most interesting and dramatic in recent major league history.

"THAT WAS a day to talk about."

In the article my father explained, "I took two strikes and after each one I held up my finger and said, 'That's one' and 'That's two.' . . . That's when I waved to the fence.

"No, I didn't point to any spot, but as long as I'd called the first two strikes on myself, I had to go through with it. It was damned foolishness, sure, but I just felt like doing it, and I felt pretty sure Root would put one close enough for me to cut at, because I was showing him up, too, wasn't I? What the hell, he had to take a chance as well as I did or walk me. Gosh, that was a great feeling."

Deane's article added that as my father was circling the bases, he thought to himself, "You lucky bum."

Daddy admitted later, "Yeah, it was silly. I was a blankety-blank fool. But I got away with it, and after Gehrig homered behind me, their backs were broken. That was a day to talk about."

Deane also reported in the article something that was news to almost everyone, including me. He said that on June 11, 1986, the controversy came before the California Court of Historic Review and Appeals, a mock court in San Francisco presided over by a real municipal court judge, Judge George Choppelas. After hearing testimony on both sides of the issue, fifty-four years after the home run, Judge Choppelas handed down a 600-word decision in which he declared:

It is not important if the incidents referred to in . . . legends really did in fact happen. What is important is that a large segment of the people believe that they did occur, and it is for us as individuals to place whatever credence or value on these stories as we might desire . . .

It is the Court's opinion that the legend of Babe Ruth pointing to the

centerfield fence shall remain intact for future generations of baseball fans
and sportswriters to argue about.

The petition before this Court to rule against the Babe Ruth legend is
therefore denied.

It remained, however, for my father's former "mascot" to hand down
what may be the most authoritative decision in the case. Speaking at the
1995 seminar at Hofstra University, Ray Kelly said emphatically that
Daddy did in fact call that shot. "I was there," Ray said, "and saw it."

Case closed.

Ray Kelly became one of my father's greatest admirers, and that appreciation of him never lessened over the years, even long after Daddy
passed away. "He was more than a hero to me for the ten years I spent
with him," he said in a television interview. "He was almost like a father.
. . . And as far as I was concerned, he always acted around me like a big
kid. He was a jovial individual, loved everybody, and particularly loved
children. He never had a bad word to say about anybody in my presence.
He was just a wonderful human being."

Other children touched by "the Babe" when he was one of the most
famous people in the world have offered similar proof of his deep and
genuine love for children. Johnny Sylvester was one of them. He was an
eleven-year-old boy who was seriously ill from either blood poisoning or
injuries suffered when he was thrown from a horse, depending on which
account of the story you heard or read.

His father wrote a letter to Daddy asking for his autograph, and
Daddy answered with a lot more: an autographed baseball, another one
signed by Rogers Hornsby (the manager of the St. Louis Cardinals who

"Yeah, it was silly. I was a blankety-blank fool. But I got away with it."

had defeated the Yankees in the 1926 World Series), and best of all, a personal visit. My father took it upon himself to drive to Essex Falls, New Jersey, to meet Johnny in his home on Roseland Avenue. Young Johnny had not been doing well, but his father later said that Johnny started getting better immediately after that visit. He called it a miracle, and the *New York Times* mentioned the visit in my father's obituary years later.

Johnny grew up to become the president of a machinery company in New York. Twenty-two years later, when my father was ill with cancer, Johnny visited him on Riverside Drive. His visit may have had the same beneficial effect as my father's had on Johnny years before. Daddy was seriously ill when Johnny visited him, but he lived for another few months after Johnny came to see him. Johnny later donated the ball my father gave him to the Babe Ruth Birthplace Museum in Baltimore, where it is still on display.

One of my father's most enthusiastic fans was the Yankees' announcer, Mel Allen, who became a Babe Ruth fan as a boy, long before he became the team's broadcaster. Mel was born in Alabama, but even living down South he was a Yankees fan, and as an announcer he had a ready explanation of how it happened. "Every summer, Mom would take the kids to visit her parents up in Detroit," he would tell audiences. On one of these summer trips, young Mel "managed to get twenty-five cents together to get into the bleachers at the then–Navin Field [home field of the Detroit Tigers]. I wanted to see the person that we thought was next to God.

"I don't remember much about the game," he admitted, "because my eyes were fixed on 'the Bambino.' And this is a true story. He was the last man to bat in the top of the eighth inning and made the final out.

The Yankees were way behind. The Tigers were retired in the last of the eighth, so now the Yankees come to bat in the top of the ninth inning, and the game is surely going to be over. The Yankees are behind by five runs.

"They had a common runway to the clubhouses in those days, and so he had to go right by the Tiger bench and down the stairs to get to the clubhouse. But instead—having made the last out of the eighth inning—he didn't expect to come to bat in the ninth. So he sits down on the Tigers' bench, and he's having one heck of a time, even though his team is behind. But that was part of Babe Ruth . . .

"And, lo and behold, the Yankees put on a rally and dadgum, the ninth batter is due up and Babe, he bursts out laughing, gets off the Tiger bench, walks around back of home plate, goes to the Yankee bench where the bats are and picks up his bat.

"There are a couple of men on base, with the Yanks still behind by two runs, and—typical of Babe Ruth's life in so many of those instances—he belts the ball over the center field fence for a home run to cap a six-run rally."

As it was for Mel Allen, the name "Babe Ruth" was tied inextricably to baseball for so many kids. And they did what they could to get closer to their hero. On the occasion of Daddy's death, former President Herbert Hoover told the story of the time a little boy approached him during his term as president and asked him for three autographs. The president said he would be happy to give the boy his autograph, but he asked why the young man needed three of them instead of just one.

"Because," the boy explained, in what he obviously considered perfect logic, "if I have three of them, I can keep one for myself and trade the other two for one of Babe Ruth."

Enclosures

TEAM PORTRAIT

Photograph of the 1927 New York Yankees signed by forty-five
members of the team, including Babe Ruth and Lou Gehrig.

PROGRAM AND TICKET

Selected program pages and ticket from Game 3 of the 1932 Yankees
vs. Cubs World Series, played at Chicago's Wrigley Field. A crowd of
nearly 50,000 saw Ruth hit his famous called-shot home run.

"NO ONE HIT HOME RUNS THE WAY BABE DID. THEY WERE SOMETHING SPECIAL. THEY WERE LIKE HOMING PIGEONS."

— Lefty Gomez, Yankees teammate

Chapter 6

GOOD WILL AMBASSADOR

OPPOSITE: Babe signs autographs for a crowd of enthusiastic young fans.

THROUGHOUT THE FIRST HALF OF THE

1930s, Ruth continued to experience tremendous success. He kept on hitting home runs, even at what most people would consider an advanced age for a professional athlete. On August 21, 1931, he hit the six hundredth home run of his career against George Blaeholder of the St. Louis Browns. He established the 700 Home Run Club three years later, on July 13, 1934, off Tommy Bridges of the Detroit Tigers. Ruth wasn't getting these home runs off third-rate pitchers, either; Bridges, for example, won 194 games in a Major League career that lasted sixteen years and included three seasons in which he was a twenty-game winner.

Ruth's exploits helped to raise the spirits of Americans during the Great Depression, and his patriotic side led him to a barnstorming tour of Japan in 1934, spreading the gospel of baseball overseas. During World War II, he used his enormous popularity to raise funds, selling war bonds and playing exhibition games. His name was known around the world, even in countries where baseball was never played.

But as his family and teammates would attest, Ruth was never one to let fame and fortune change him.

Despite his growing popularity, Daddy never seemed to let things alter who he was as a person. He always maintained a happy, positive attitude, and his love for the people in his world—especially the kids—and his all-around enthusiasm for life were obvious to anyone who met him.

He kept his good-natured view of the world throughout everything that comes with being famous, including the wildest requests from

BELOW: Up to bat in an exhibition game during a barnstorming tour of Japan in 1934. Ruth's fame spread around the world, creating hordes of new baseball fans. The Japanese Baseball League formed two years later, in 1936.

fans. Once he received a letter from a boy asking for, of all things, a lock of his hair. That's not exactly something a boy typically writes to a professional athlete about—but Daddy made sure to write back:

Dear Mathew,

In all my years in baseball, I have received many requests for autographs, bats, balls and equipment, but you are the first person to ask me for some of my hair. Therefore, I feel I am obliged to comply with such a request, at least once. You will find enclosed an envelope containing some of my hair. I don't know what you're going to do with it, but I hope you enjoy it. Good luck with your collection.

Sincerely,

Babe Ruth

He extended his role as baseball's goodwill ambassador in 1934, two years after hitting his "called-shot" home run. This time it was on a barnstorming tour of Japan with a team of fourteen baseball All-Stars, including some of the biggest names in the game at that time: Jimmie Foxx, Lefty Gomez, Earl Averill, Charlie Gehringer, and Lou Gehrig. In all, they played a series of twenty-two games during their tour. My mother and I were lucky enough to travel along with them.

Japanese sportswriter Kazuo Sayama credited my dad with spreading not only his own popularity but the popularity of baseball itself across the seas. "He accelerated the formation of the professional baseball league in Japan," Sayama said. "He was the father.

"When he came to Japan in 1934, the first thing he did was to spend some time with the children," Sayama continued. "They were at the pier, the Yokohama Pier. They were lined up in baseball uniforms. And the first thing Babe did was to talk to them, play with them, you know, and carry them in his arms. And not only that, he encouraged other baseball players, American players, to do the same. The first thing he showed was his love for the children, his love for the Japanese, and we all loved him."

While in Japan, my father generated even more enthusiasm from the crowds—the adults as well as the kids—by riding in an open car, waving

ABOVE: Babe poses with a group of uniformed boys during his 1934 barnstorming tour of Japan. He was a major factor in the rise of baseball's popularity around the world, especially in Japan.

RIGHT: The sight of Ruth riding in an open car generates enthusiasm from a crowd in Japan. Waving an American flag in one hand and a Japanese flag in the other, Ruth passed along his love for baseball to the Japanese people.

an American flag in one hand and a Japanese flag in the other. As Sayama explained, "Before that [visit], you know, we had a very strict and rigid idea of this sport. We took it too seriously, and he taught us how to enjoy. He taught us the enjoyment of baseball. And after that, the same idea prevailed all over Japan."

When my father took me on that barnstorming trip, it was his present to me for graduating from high school. And he didn't limit it to Japan; he turned it into an around-the-world tour for the three of us. In my case, he gave me a choice—going to college or seeing the world, literally. I chose the trip. In the 1930s, there wasn't the emphasis on women attending college that we began to see in the 1940s after World War II, and I think any other seventeen-year-old—boy or girl—would have made the same decision at the time.

We toured England, France, and other countries in Europe as well as Japan and other nations in the Far East. I convinced myself that the whole experience was much more of an education than I would have received in a college classroom, and I still believe that was a valid attitude, especially in those years. The trip gave me an opportunity that doesn't exist anymore: to see the world as it was before World War II reshaped it. Even the names of some of the countries we visited were changed as a result of the war.

My father was approaching the end of his career as a player when that 1934 barnstorming trip ended. Before the next season began, he became a free agent, and Emil Fuchs, the owner of the Boston Braves, signed him to a contract for 1935. It was hard for him to leave the Yankees after so many years, and hard for the fans to let him go. By that time, Yankee Stadium was almost like a home, and the Yankees his family.

"Whether you were a fan or an employee, you would feel his presence. You always had an appreciation for the fact that— wow!—this is where Babe Ruth played."

Marty Appel, the former public relations director for the Yankees, can bear witness to my father's lasting popularity in New York. The continuing effects of his giant personality have always been more evident at Yankee Stadium than anywhere else, from the day he christened the brand new ballpark in 1923 with its first home run right up to the present.

"You would go there each day, whether you were a fan or an employee," Marty remembered a few years ago, "and you would feel the presence of Babe Ruth. There were photographs, there was the monument in deep center field, there's a huge smokestack outside the stadium in the plaza that's in the shape of a bat with his name on it. But you always had a grand appreciation for the fact that—wow!—this is where Babe Ruth played. And I think that will forever be part of Yankee Stadium."

Another part of Yankee Stadium is a pre-game ritual by Yankees pitching star Roger Clemens, who visits the monuments in the outfield before each game in which he's scheduled to pitch and wipes sweat from his brow onto the monument to my father.

The legacy of those monuments and the untold stories and rituals surrounding Yankee Stadium and my father are undergoing changes as of this writing. A new Yankee Stadium is being built to replace the present one and will be completed for the 2009 season. Groundbreaking took place on August 16, 2006, the fifty-eighth anniversary of Daddy's death, and construction began the next day. The new stadium will be located just north of the present ballpark, between 161st and 164th Streets, between Jerome and River Avenues, across the street from the present Yankee Stadium. It will feature the same dimensions, fences, and latticework as its predecessor. The original Yankee Stadium, owned by New York City, will become a park for the city's youth. The new ballpark will be an open-air structure with a grass field that seats 51,800 fans, built at a cost of $1.02 billion.

BELOW: Standing with a group of children from St. Ann's Home in Tacoma, Washington, 1926.

Marty elaborated on his explanation of my father's popularity, even among people who were born after he passed away. "Babe Ruth's popularity, I believe, endures because of his personality more than his feats on the field," he said. "Particularly his love for children and the fact that he, himself, came out of such a difficult childhood, out of a reform school upbringing, thrust into professional baseball while still a babe. . . . And those charming newsreel photographs of him with children, and his personality just kind of overwhelming the game."

Bob Feller, the Hall of Fame pitcher for the Cleveland Indians, had a similar explanation, expressed from a player's point of view. "The players

liked him," Bob said. "He was always giving them a laugh. Babe loved to have people around him. There are some people who are loners and some people that can't go without having people around them. We all know that. And we have it on ball clubs. We have it in any walk of life. And Babe wanted people around him."

Despite his love of life and everyone in it, my father still couldn't shake one lifelong difficulty—remembering names. He was the world's worst when it came to remembering names, which simply added to the affection that people felt for him. He got around his problem by calling every young player "Kid," and every veteran "Doc." That worked, except for the time when one of his closest friends on the Yankees, Waite Hoyt, his teammate for ten years, was traded to the Detroit Tigers. My father said an emotional goodbye to him. His teammates could hear him as he told his close friend, "I'm going to miss you, Kid. Take care of yourself—uh—uh—Walter." The dressing room exploded with the laughter of their teammates.

Patriotism was also a prominent part of my father's personality. He was as patriotic as any American, and he showed it when the Japanese attacked Pearl Harbor. On that evening, he was so furious at the Japanese leaders that he lost his temper at the thought that any nation could do a thing like that. He grabbed a handful of souvenirs from our 1934 trip to Japan and threw them out the window of our Riverside Drive apartment, sending awards and gifts hurtling fourteen floors down and right into Riverside Park.

He was too old for service in the armed forces during the war—forty-six—so he made as many appearances as he could to promote the sale of war bonds and visit with our service men and women. Americans bought

RIGHT: Preparing to tee off at a golf fundraiser for the British War Relief Fund and the United Service Organizations in the summer of 1941. Ruth played against fellow Hall of Famer and longtime rival on the diamond Ty Cobb.

OPPOSITE: Cobb and Ruth at the golf fundraiser. Cobb was the victor, winning two games out of three.

some $59,369,000,000 in bonds to help pay for the war, and my father raised more than his share of those sales with his many public appearances.

Even before the United States entered the war, my father began his work as a fundraiser for our allies. In the summer of 1941, his newfound love for golf in his retirement led him to a three-game series against his old baseball rival, Ty Cobb (Cobb won two out of three). All of the proceeds were donated to the British War Relief Fund and the United Service Organizations.

On August 23, 1942, at Yankee Stadium, he faced Walter Johnson on the field for the last time, before a Yankees-Senators game. They were raising money for the Army and Navy Relief Fund, to help support the women and children who were widowed and orphaned by the war. During the game, Daddy hit a home run that landed in his favorite spot—the right field seats. After the exhibition, a reporter asked Walter Johnson, truly one of the nicest people in the history of baseball, why he had "grooved"

RIGHT: Batting against Walter Johnson during a war bonds fundraising game at Yankee Stadium in 1942. (Ruth hit a home run.) Seven years after his final season in the Major Leagues, Ruth's appearance on the baseball diamond continued to attract droves of fans.

the pitch to my father. Walter replied, "The fans didn't come here to see me strike out Babe Ruth. They came to see him hit a home run."

His popularity was so well known around the world that his name even came up among the soldiers and marines fighting in the Pacific. Japanese snipers hiding in foxholes on the islands there would holler, "To hell with Babe Ruth!" It was their way of trying to make the American G.I.'s angry enough to stick their heads out of their own hiding places to try to take a shot at them—but I've never heard anyone say their trick worked.

Later in the war, my father made an appearance in Washington that surprised practically everyone but the man who arranged it, Shirley Povich, an award-winning sports columnist for the *Washington Post.* The event was an exhibition game between the Senators and a team of navy all-stars including Bob Feller, Phil Rizzuto, and Dom DiMaggio.

Povich showed himself to be a star producer by lining up two of America's most popular singers of those years, Kate Smith and Bing Crosby. Smith stood behind second base and sang the country's newest smash hit, *God Bless America,* and Crosby sang some of his biggest songs. Then, for the big finish, Daddy trotted out of the Senators dugout on the first base side, waved to the crowd, and jogged around the bases. When the fans roared for him, they were also roaring for America. We badly needed something to cheer about in those days.

In the end, the event raised about two million dollars, enough to pay for a navy cruiser, and the second largest amount of money to be raised through a sporting event up until then. (Only the second Dempsey-Tunney boxing match had brought in more.) Every one of those performers had a hand in raising those two million dollars, and my father's personality was certainly a factor in the evening's success.

Chapter 7

PROVEN GREAT NESS

OPPOSITE: Ruth, shown in his Braves uniform in 1935, played for the Boston team for one year, his final season in the Major Leagues.

BABE RUTH SPENT HIS LAST SEASON

as a professional player with the Boston Braves, after being given his un-conditional release from the Yankees. Although '35 was no '27, he went out on a high note, with three home runs in his second-to-last game. He was the first player over forty years of age to hit three home runs in one game, and is still one of only three players over forty to do so (the other two are Stan Musial and Reggie Jackson).

In 1939, when the Baseball Hall of Fame opened, Ruth belonged to the first "class" of twenty-five players inducted. On the one hundredth an-niversary of professional baseball's beginning, he was voted the Greatest Player Ever, and in 1998, the baseball bible the Sporting News *ranked him number one on the list of "Baseball's 100 Greatest Players." Perhaps even more telling is the fact that the men he played with and against hold him up as the greatest of all time.*

I hope I don't sound too much like a bragging daughter here. Any daughter would be proud of what my father accomplished and of his immense popularity all over the world. Besides, as the saying goes, numbers don't lie. And if you don't believe the numbers, you can believe the statements of those other great men who played with and against him.

My father played while baseball was still an all-white sport, but he got the chance to play with African American players in exhibition games. One of them later became the first African American coach in the Major Leagues: Buck O'Neill, a first baseman for the Kansas City Monarchs and a fellow goodwill ambassador for the sport. O'Neill recalled with fondness the time my father played against another great African American player, future Hall of Famer Satchel Paige, during the barnstorming exhibition games of the 1930s.

BELOW: Hall of Fame pitcher Satchel Paige warms up. Paige and Ruth faced off in popular integrated exhibition games between Major League and Negro League players.

"After Babe was out of baseball, he would go to different cities because he was quite a draw," O'Neill said during a 1995 interview. "So he played against Kansas City, and they billed it as 'Satchel Paige against Babe Ruth.' And oh, people were all over the place."

"We had to make ground rules," he continued. "Hit the ball in the crowd and it was a double, and the first pitch Satchel threw Babe Ruth, Babe Ruth hit—it must have been 500 feet . . . They had those wind breakers out in right field where they grew high cedars, and he hit the ball over them. And as he rounded the bases, Satchel looked at him, and when he got to home plate, Satchel was there to congratulate him. . . . They held up the ballgame five minutes for a kid to go out, get the ball, and bring it back so Ruth could autograph the ball for Satchel."

O'Neill compared the two immortal baseball stars by saying, "Both men were great. When you say 'greatness,' you don't need anything else to add. You're great, you're great. This is what a lot of people do. When you are great, they say you're one of the best. You're reputed to be the best. But when you're great, you're great. It's when you come up with Ruth, you come up with Josh Gibson [one of the home run stars of the Negro Leagues], you come up with Satchel. You just say 'great.'"

My father joined the Boston Braves of the National League for the 1935 season. In saying goodbye to New York and his teammates and the city's fans, he could look back on fifteen years as a Yankee during which he hit 659 home runs, compiled a batting average of .349, and drove in 1,959 runs. All of those marks still stand as team records.

On April 16, he was the starting left fielder for the Braves in his first game at Braves Field since he pitched for the Red Sox in the 1916

LEFT: Babe pictured with a member of the New York Giants, Bill Terry. The Braves played the Giants in the opening game of the 1935 season and went on to defeat them 4–2 after Ruth hit a home run in the fifth inning, his first playing in the National League.

World Series. A capacity crowd of 25,000 fans showed up, including no fewer than five governors of New England states, despite temperatures dipping to 39 degrees. No doubt many of them were attracted by the presence of Daddy in a Braves uniform. And, you guessed it—in the bottom half of the fifth inning, he hit his first National League home run. His new team went on to defeat his former New York rivals, the Giants, 4–2.

RIGHT: Ruth crosses the plate, scoring one of his runs against the Giants on Opening Day at Braves Field in Boston on April 16, 1935.

RIGHT: Ruth hit six home runs for the Braves, including one in the opening game of the season. He knocked out the final three home runs of his career during his second-to-last ever Major League game.

He wasn't through hitting home runs just yet. On May 25, he hit the 712th, 713th, and 714th home runs of his career at Forbes Field in Pittsburgh. By this time he was forty years old, and his homers would be the final three of his career. But the last was truly one for the memory books—indeed, "Ruthian" in more ways than one. Home run number 714 sailed over the roof at Forbes, making him the first player to knock one out of that ballpark. As the Associated Press reported, it was "a prodigious clout that carried clear over the right field grandstand, bounded into the street and rolled into Schenley Park."

Five days later, Daddy played in his last Major League game. At that time, his 714 home runs were more than double the amount of the second-place home run hitter, Lou Gehrig.

My father commanded so much respect for his ability and accomplishments that some people have even said he could have been baseball's only hitter with a *lifetime* batting average over .400, which would have been more than thirty points higher than the highest ever recorded, Ty Cobb's .367 lifetime average. They say all he would have needed to do to accomplish such an unimaginable feat would have been to be content with more singles and doubles and fewer home runs. But the fans didn't come out to see my father hit singles, and he knew it. He was quoted once as saying, "If I had just tried for those dinky singles, I could have hit .600."

Marty Appel, a walking authority on everything Babe Ruth because of his work with the Yankees, once said in a television interview, "One could argue that he was the greatest baseball player because he had the opportunity to show his abilities as both a pitcher and as a hitter.

Others, of course, never had that opportunity. They immediately entered the Major Leagues as one or the other. So from a statistical and historical point of view, yes, you can make the claim for Ruth, without knowing about what others might have done."

Marty went further, suggesting that my father might even have been the greatest American athlete in any sport. He explained his reasoning by saying, "If one says that baseball players are more gifted than athletes in other sports, then one would say Babe Ruth was the greatest athlete of all time. I'm not sure any of us could make that argument with any certainty. I think he was the greatest *baseball player* who ever lived. And if baseball players are more gifted because of the skills required in their game, then clearly he was the best athlete America ever produced. Certainly by the force of his personality, he was the most *important* athlete ever produced in America."

My son, Tom Stevens, heard testimony from one of my father's fellow Hall of Famers, Joe Sewell, who was his teammate as a third baseman for the Yankees in 1931, 1932, and 1933. He said Joe told him of a time when Daddy was having trouble putting his uniform on. Tom said he was taking medication for an injury, and it was making him "dopey." He was also limping. So Joe helped him on with his uniform.

Then Tom told the rest of the story: "In spite of his condition, he still managed to go 3-for-4 with two home runs and five runs batted in. At that point, Mr. Sewell looked up at me with a twinkle in his eye and said, 'Son, your grandfather was a baseball god.'"

Even many years after the fact, the men who played with my father and against him always gave him rave reviews in describing his greatness as a player, as a team man, and as a great person to have on the

RIGHT: Shaking hands with Frank Crosetti on October 23, 1931. A shortstop for the Yankees during Ruth's final three years with the team, Crosetti admired Ruth and credited him for igniting public interest in the sport like never before.

field, in the dugout, and in the clubhouse. Frankie Crosetti, the outstanding Yankee shortstop during my father's years there, said flatly, "He did more for baseball than anybody ever did or ever will do. After the Black Sox scandal, he brought people back. People think something is crooked and they're not going to go, right? Then along comes this guy hitting home runs, and the people listen to him on the radio because there's no TV then, and they finally say, 'Let's go see this guy hit those home runs.'"

Then Frankie added, "He once told me, 'Every time I go to bat, I try to hit a home run, because I know the people come out to see me hit a home run.'"

Mel Harder, an All-Star pitcher for the Cleveland Indians, said, "You had to be careful with him on everything you threw. I tried to pitch to spots and go in and out. When he hit it, it looked like a golf ball."

Al Lopez, a Hall of Fame catcher, said, "I'm not knocking the other guys, but I think if I had to pick the one player that I think was the greatest player of them all, I'd have to take Babe Ruth, because he not only was a great outfielder and a home run hitter, but he would have been a Hall of Famer as a pitcher. He was a great pitcher—the best in the league at the time."

And Harry "The Hat" Walker said his brother, Dixie, a star outfielder for the Brooklyn Dodgers, told him that my father had the best instincts playing the game of anybody. Harry said, "When he got the ball, he knew where it had to go. Dixie said the man was uncanny, and that he ran a lot better than people thought. You know, he stole 123 bases. This man was the greatest ballplayer who ever played, in my book."

"When he got the ball, he knew where it had to go. The man was uncanny."

LEFT: Sliding to the plate on March 3, 1927. Though some might not guess it from his stature in later years, the home run king was much faster than people think; he stole 123 bases in his career, and stole home ten times.

Babe Ruth and Lou Gehrig pose with Miller Huggins (center), manager of the Yankees until his death in 1929. Ruth had dreams of succeeding Huggins as manager, but was never given the opportunity.

Robert W. Creamer, who wrote a popular biography called *Babe: The Legend Comes to Life,* noted in his book that my father's name is frequently used to denote excellence and great achievement in a particular undertaking. He said when Willie Sutton, the notorious convicted bank robber, was released from prison, *Time* magazine called him "the Babe Ruth of bank robbers." The *New York Times* described Enrico Caruso, an internationally acclaimed singer during Daddy's years, as "the Babe Ruth of operatic tenors." Even in more recent times, the owner of the Chicago Bulls, Jerry Reinsdorf, said Michael Jordan, the basketball star, was "the Babe Ruth of the NBA." And Bruce Springsteen has been described as "the Babe Ruth of rock."

Poet Ogden Nash, with his impish sense of humor, measured Daddy's towering personality in the poem "Lineup for Yesterday" by describing him in only four lines:

R is for Ruth.

To tell you the truth,

There's no more to be said,

Just R is for Ruth.

Yet in spite of my father's incredible talents on the field, somehow the men who ran things never had enough faith in his ability to *lead* a team. When the manager of the Yankees, Miller Huggins, died on September 25, 1929, Daddy had hopes of being named manager to succeed Huggins, but the job went to his former teammate on the Yankees pitching staff, Bob Shawkey, instead. Shawkey held the position for only one year before being replaced by Joe McCarthy for the 1931 season, after the Yankees finished in third place.

"He had the reputation of being a smart baseball man. Other players and some managers and coaches said he never threw to the wrong base."

My father's disappointment in not becoming a manager was bad enough that first time, but to make matters worse it happened to him twice more, and the culprit in both cases was Larry MacPhail. Daddy said MacPhail promised him the job as manager of the Brooklyn Dodgers in the 1930s but then passed him over. MacPhail did it again in 1946, when he hired Bucky Harris to succeed Joe McCarthy. Daddy said later, "Nobody knows what kind of manager I would have made. Today I'm not sore at anybody, but I still think I should have had my chance. Speaker and Cobb had theirs, and I guess it was natural that I should expect a crack at managing some day. But I didn't, and that's that."

At the time, he must have sensed that baseball had passed him by and would continue to do so. After he got that second rejection from MacPhail, Daddy went into our living room. Then he sat down and cried.

All of us hate to see our parents become disappointed because of a job they didn't get or something else that didn't go their way. I'm still convinced that he would have been an excellent manager, in part simply because of his sharp knowledge of baseball. He didn't often bring the game home with him, but occasionally he'd be upset because he felt the Yankees could have won by doing a few things differently. He would launch into an analysis saying, "If we had done this or that, we would've won that game." He had the reputation of being a smart baseball man. Other players and some managers and coaches said he never threw to the wrong base, was never out of position in the outfield, was a smart pitcher, and was one of the most intelligent players of his era.

Of course, it was known throughout baseball that my father always enjoyed a good time. That was a key part of his makeup. As his friend, columnist and co-writer of his autobiography Bob Considine, described in

the book, my father "thought every night was New Year's Eve." But Bob was quick to add that he "could still rise the next day to phenomenal feats on the diamond."

I believe, more than anything, that reputation for thinking every night was New Year's Eve—for loving the bright lights and the good times too much—is what led people to conclude he wouldn't make a good baseball manager. Unfair as it was, upon his retirement as an active player, many doubted his ability to control an entire team because they assumed

ABOVE: Sitting with Larry MacPhail, the executive who, despite his promises, twice passed over Ruth for management positions. MacPhail did offer Ruth a job coaching first base, which he took, but after finding it a far cry from management, Ruth quit at the end of the season.

he couldn't control himself. But the fact is that he *could* handle himself. Bob Feller got it right when he said, "He did drink and he did stay out late at night . . . but at that age when you're that young, in your twenties, you can go out and take a shower and keep going. It's not going to bother you if you don't do it all the time. . . . I presume Babe was smart enough to know when he'd had enough and would get a couple of good nights' sleep and stay off the booze."

If it's any indication of how well he would control twenty-five players, he handled Dorothy and me like an expert disciplinarian. He was not a harsh father, but he was strict enough to make sure we behaved. Like any kid, I didn't appreciate his "management style" when I was growing up, but when I became a parent myself, I could see that what I was doing in raising my son, Tom, were the very same things my father did in raising me, right down to the specific rules I put in place for when he should be home and how he should behave.

When I was a teenager, Daddy would tell me before I went out on a date, in the clearest terms, "Now, you have to be home by midnight." Further, the rule continued to apply to me until the day I got married. And, yes, my dates made sure to get me home on time. That strict-but-fair approach even prompted my father to force me to break an engagement with a nice young man when I was twenty years old, based on his firm belief that "no girl has enough sense to get married until she's twenty-five years old." I'll grant that he was speaking from experience—he married his first wife, Helen, when he was twenty, and it didn't work out, and in Mother's case, she was a teenager when she married for the first time, and that one didn't pan out either. As a result, Daddy honestly believed it was best for me to wait until I was twenty-five before listening for wedding bells.

"He honestly believed it was best for me to wait until I was twenty-five before listening for wedding bells."

In the end, I was twenty-three when I heard them. My father, who was always so fair with me, must have decided to give me the benefit of the doubt.

BELOW: Ruth jokingly points a bat at his new son-in-law on the day of Julia's wedding to Richard Flanders.

—— *Enclosures* ——

"R" IS FOR RUTH

In this A–Z of baseball by poet Ogden Nash, Ruth falls
alphabetically into the lineup.

FIVE-CENT SCORECARD

Scorecard from Opening Day at Braves Field in Boston, April 16,
1935. Ruth is listed third in the batting order.

PITTSBURGH PRESS, MAY 26, 1935

Front page of the *Pittsburgh Press* sports section the day after Ruth
hit the last home runs of his career.

"HE WAS BETTER THAN ME. HE WAS THE BEST THAT EVER LIVED. THAT BIG JOKER HIT IT CLEAR OUT OF THE PARK."

Chapter 8

SAYING
GOODBYE

THROUGH 1947 AND 1948, RUTH FOUND

himself in and out of hospitals. He didn't know at the time that he was suffering from cancer. Nevertheless, he got out whenever he could to show his fans that he was still kicking. April 27, 1947, was declared Babe Ruth Day in his honor at every Major League ballpark, and in May he established the Babe Ruth Foundation, Inc., to help underprivileged youth. His last public appearance came on Yankee Stadium's twenty-fifth anniversary in 1948. A huge ovation from 49,641 fans celebrated the last time the number 3 was worn by any Yankee; after that day, Ruth's number was officially retired.

My father began to suffer from severe pain over his left eye in 1946, along with headaches, hoarseness, and difficulty in swallowing. He was admitted to French Hospital in New York in November, where doctors discovered a malignant tumor in his neck. He was operated on and then underwent radiation treatments. He lost eighty pounds in just three months before being released from the hospital in February of 1947. He also received some thirty thousand letters during his stay.

The news was bad enough, but there was a bright spot. In the chemotherapy field, a new development seemed to offer a ray of hope. A new drug called teropterin had been developed and doctors were starting to introduce it as part of the chemotherapy treatment. In the early returns, it was producing significant remissions in children with leukemia. Daddy was given the drug in June 1947 after his symptoms returned. He agreed to try this new medicine, but he told us he didn't want anyone to know about it. During the time he was receiving this drug, which was still experimental, he never knew it was for the treatment of cancer.

He began receiving injections on June 19, 1947, and the improvement in his condition was immediate and dramatic. He gained more than twenty pounds, and his headaches subsided. Almost three months later, on September 6, his case was presented anonymously at a cancer session in St. Louis. Doctors understand now that my father was suffering from a rare kind of tumor in the back of the nose near the Eustachian tube.

A 1948 newspaper article reported, "In the early months of treatment last year, the drug produced what doctors described as a 'remarkable' improvement in Ruth's condition, although it did not seem to be so effective in other cases."

OPPOSITE: Yankees manager Bucky Harris (left) and a team batboy pal around with Ruth in the dugout on Babe Ruth Day, 1947.

The article continued, "There was great excitement in the medical profession at the time, and doctors throughout the nation came to know of Ruth as medical science's best example of teropterin therapy in cancer. His improvement gave the medical profession the world over hope that cancer could be combated successfully by the simple administration of a drug."

Upon commissioner of baseball A. B. Happy Chandler's declaration that April 27, 1947, was Babe Ruth Day, ceremonies were held in every one of the sixteen big-league ballparks. The most significant one of them all, of course, was at Yankee Stadium.

It was a rainy and chilly April Sunday, and my father appeared in his trademark clothing—a camel hair coat with a cap to match. The master of ceremonies was an obvious choice—the Yankees' own Mel Allen. "When he was finally introduced," Mel remembered, "the fans sent up a din the likes of which I never heard, and it kept on and on and on and on."

Mel was in a difficult situation. "What a lot of people don't know," he said years later, "and even I might have misunderstood, was that Babe couldn't talk. You know, he'd had this operation that affected his vocal cords. But the ovation was so tremendous, I put my lips to Babe's ear and I said, 'Babe, do you want to try to say something?' And in his croaked fashion, whatever he had left for a voice, he said, 'I must—'"

After Mel introduced him, my father spoke hoarsely, struggling to make himself heard. It must have taken a maximum effort on his part, but, like the champion he always was, he rose to the occasion. He leaned toward the microphone and said in his strained voice:

"Thank you very much, ladies and gentlemen. You know how bad my voice sounds. Well, it feels just as bad. You know, this baseball game of

ours comes up from the youth. That means the boys. And after you've been a boy and grow up to know how to play ball, then you come to the boys who are representing themselves today in our national pastime. The only real game in the world, I think, is baseball.

"As a rule, some people think if you give them a football or a baseball or something like that, naturally they're athletes right away. But you can't do that in baseball. You've got to start from way down at the bottom when you're six or seven years old. You can't wait until you're fifteen or sixteen. You've got to let it grow up with you. And if you're successful and you try hard enough, you're bound to come out on top, just like all these boys.

"There have been so many lovely things said about me here today. I'm glad I had the opportunity to thank everybody."

Daddy continued his courageous battle against his cancer, and a year later, on June 13, 1948, he made his last appearance at Yankee Stadium. The date marked the stadium's twenty-fifth anniversary, and as part of the celebration, a special two-inning exhibition game was held prior to the scheduled game (Yankees versus Indians). My father, wearing the familiar pinstripes with his number 3 on the back, got to manage a team of reunited 1923 Yankees, including such greats as Waite Hoyt, Bob Meusel, Sad Sam Jones, and Bob Shawkey. He led them to a 2–0 win against the younger New York veterans comprising the other exhibition team.

The Yankees retired my father's number that day, and he donated his uniform to the Baseball Hall of Fame. This appearance would be his goodbye, and every person in that ballpark, including Daddy, knew it. Cleveland starting pitcher Bob Feller would later describe the emotional scene as he remembered it:

"Babe Ruth came walking down what was a common runway, because in those days the clubhouses were in the same runway, the third base runway. Babe came in, and he kind of stumbled a little bit. We went up the steps, and Eddie Robinson, our first baseman, grabbed a bat—it happened to be my bat—and gave it to Babe. And he walked up to home plate with it and leaned on it, kind of like a cane or a crutch. And, of course, he spoke to the fans with his very raspy voice because he had throat cancer.

LEFT: Babe is met with a standing ovation on June 13, 1948, during Yankee Stadium's twenty-fifth anniversary celebration. At the event, the Yankees officially retired his uniform number, 3.

Babe came back and autographed the bat for Eddie Robinson, and he said, 'This bat feels pretty good.' Robinson said, 'Babe, it should. It's a Babe Ruth model.'" Feller ended the interview by adding proudly, "That bat is in my museum in Van Meter, Iowa."

As my father stood at home plate in his old pinstripes, hat in hand, photographer Nat Fein caught the moment—and later won the Pulitzer Prize for that photo.

My father had one more special public tribute to enjoy. On July 26, 1948, he was able to attend the premiere of a Hollywood movie about his life, *The Babe Ruth Story,* starring William Bendix. Not long after that, he returned to the hospital for the last time. There he was visited by the mayor of New York, William O'Dwyer, and he received a telephone call from President Truman.

Less than a month later, Daddy passed away after his long, brave fight.

As far as we could tell, he never knew he had cancer, and neither did Mother. I called her early in his illness and asked her, "What's wrong with Daddy?"

Her answer was, "They don't seem to know."

Even when he checked into the Sloan-Kettering Memorial Hospital for Cancer and Allied Diseases in 1948, only a few months before he died, he asked those around him, "What are they bringing me in here for?"

He passed away on August 16, 1948. Jack Lait, the editor of the *New York Daily Mirror,* wrote later, "Every newspaperman in New York knew for years that Babe Ruth had cancer of the throat, yet that was never written. We knew he did not suspect it, and [we] feared that the dreaded word would break him down."

The writers and sportscasters maintained a voluntary silence about my father's illness, keeping it out of the papers and off the air. It sounds hard to believe today, with the never-ending race to get your story out before the competition, but in those years it happened more than once. The media's restraint here was a convincing testimony to the amount of respect and love they had for my father.

In his last hours, a group of almost one hundred children maintained a vigil outside Memorial Hospital Center for Cancer and Allied Diseases. Eventually, a priest named Father Thomas Kaufman, who had given Daddy the last rites of the Catholic church, told the reporters who were covering the story what those final hours were like.

"He said his prayers," Father Kaufman said, "and lapsed into a sleep. He died in his sleep." When he did, Daddy joined the two men he admired so much, Brother Matthias and Brother Gilbert. The three of them died within four years of each other.

Americans everywhere and from every walk of life mourned my father's death. ABC and NBC broadcast half-hour-long radio tributes, and President Truman even issued a message of sympathy. My father lay in state in the rotunda at Yankee Stadium, and 75,000 fans filed past his casket from five o'clock in the evening until seven o'clock the next morning. The line never seemed to end, or even to grow shorter. His funeral was held at St. Patrick's Cathedral, where the funerals for so many other dignitaries from American life have been conducted. One estimate said 6,500 mourners attended the Mass celebrated by Francis Cardinal Spellman. On the other side of the world, every baseball game in Japan was stopped for one minute as a silent tribute to the one the Japanese people called "Babu Russu."

Daddy was buried at Gate of Heaven cemetery in Mount Pleasant, New York. Mother lived for another twenty-eight years at their apartment on Riverside Drive, and when she passed away in 1976, she was buried next to him. To this day, people still leave messages, flowers, American flags, and baseball memorabilia at the graves of my parents.

In Hollywood, some of the writers who were with him the previous year filming *The Babe Ruth Story* remembered what he'd said when someone asked him whether he would live his life differently if he had the opportunity to live it over again. The writers said my father never hesitated in giving his answer. He told them, "I wouldn't change a thing. Let it stand. I did it. I'd probably do it again the same way."

In his autobiography, Daddy made reference to the 1919 Black Sox scandal that so many have given him credit for helping the nation forget. "If my home run hitting in 1920 established a new era in baseball, and helped the fans of the nation to forget the past and the terrible fact that they had been sold out, that's all the epitaph I want."

OPPOSITE: Fans line up to pay their last respects to Babe, who lay in state in the rotunda at Yankee Stadium, August 18, 1948.

Enclosures

NEWS OF THE REDS, APRIL 27, 1947

Special Babe Ruth Edition of the Cincinnati Reds' publication,
News of the Reds, distributed on Babe Ruth Day.

MOVIE PROGRAM, 1948

Program for *The Babe Ruth Story* featuring photos, cast list, and
details about the film score.

"HE NEVER LET THEM DOWN, NOT ONCE. HE WAS THE GREATEST CROWD PLEASER OF THEM ALL."

— Waite Hoyt, Yankees teammate

RIGHT: June 3, 1925, Yankee Stadium: Babe Ruth in his element.

ACKNOWLEDGMENTS

We owe our special thanks to several people for their interest and support while we wrote this book.

We are indebted to Mike Gibbons, the executive director of the Babe Ruth Museum in Baltimore; Greg Schwalenberg and Shawn Herne, the Museum's Curators; Lindsay Hebert, the Museum's Manager of Communications; Kjersti Egerdahl and Amy Wideman, our editors at becker&mayer! Books in Seattle; our agents, Pete Enfield, vice president of Curtis Management Group in Indianapolis, and B.G. Dilworth, president of the B.G. Dilworth Agency in New York; and the many others who have been kind enough to encourage us to write this book.

We are grateful to all of them and to our families for their interest, support, and patience while we worked on this project as a special salute to a special person—Babe Ruth.

Julia Ruth Stevens and Bill Gilbert

OPPOSITE: Babe entertains a rapt audience of young fans, November 29, 1924.

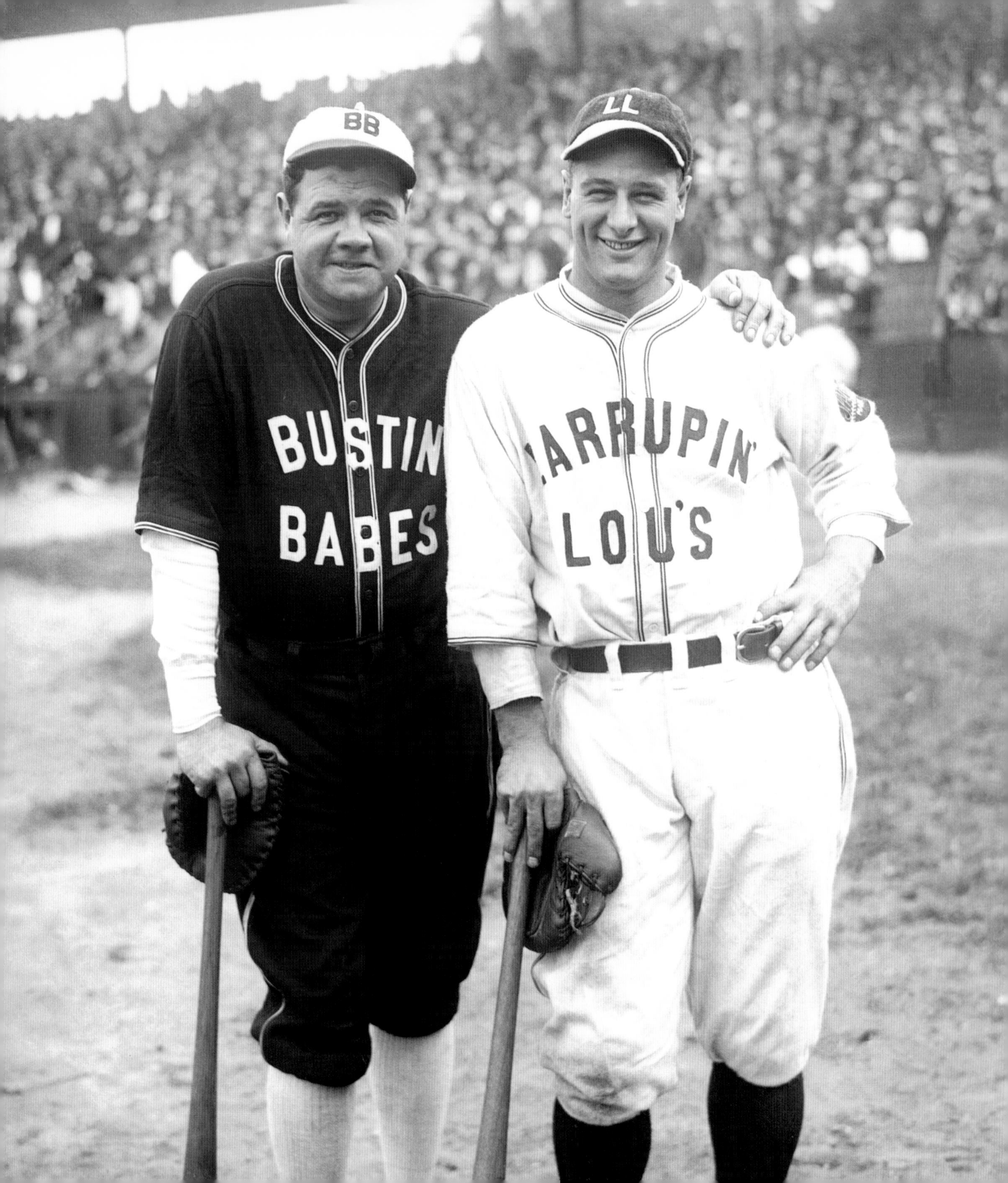
BB
BUSTIN
BABES
LL
LARRUPIN'
LOU'S

IMAGE CREDITS

Every effort has been made to trace copyright holders. If any unintended omissions have been made, becker&mayer! would be pleased to add appropriate acknowledgment in future editions.

OPPOSITE: Ruth and Gehrig swung for, respectively, the "Bustin' Babes" and the "Larrupin' Lous" during a 1927 exhibition tour.